Auto Claims Step by Step

Non-injury

Joseph E. Green

ISBN: 1979250707
ISBN-13: 978-1979250702

DEDICATION

This book is dedicated to all the people who helped me in my claims career. They helped with the good stuff. The mistakes, as always, are my own.

CONTENTS

ACKNOWLEDGMENTS

Thanks for my patient and loving wife, Dr. Faith Harper, who put up with me writing this thing.

INTRODUCTION

Hi. My name is Joe Green. I've been working in and out of the casualty insurance industry for about twenty years. I've worked physical damage claims and serious injury claims. I've worked as a private investigator, a field adjuster, a claims supervisor, and a trainer. I haven't seen it all – claims is the sort of enterprise where *nobody* has seen it all – but I've been around the block a few times.

This book came about while I was working a contract gig for a small insurance company. The office was so tiny there was only one receptionist, who hadn't worked in a claims environment before but was very bright and interested. We were talking one day and I saw her scrolling through the internet looking for a general guide to claims. She couldn't find one that looked appealing to her. I said, "OK, I'll write one." A couple months later, I began the project. You are now holding the result of that work.

I wanted to do a few things with this book. On the one hand, this is an overview guide to handling automobile damage claims. (Actual processes can and will vary depending on the insurance company.) On the other hand, this can also be used to help you if you end up in an accident. Throughout this book, you will find general tips for how the process should work if you get hit by somebody.

The main thing I wanted to do, though, was try to provide some good information to "fill in the blanks" for young adjusters. In my experience, I have noticed that claims adjusters may sometimes know *what* a given process is but not understand *why* they are following a particular process. This book will hopefully help you find the why.

Why is that important? For one thing, when you become a property and casualty adjuster, you acquire a professional designation that is distinct from the company you work for. That means you have personal responsibility. That means you have some direct control over your career. It also means you could be sued *personally* for unethical conduct. You're a professional and an expert.

If you don't understand what ethical conduct is in terms of insurance, you might unwittingly find yourself engaging in **actionable conduct**. (An activity is considered *actionable* if it could be the basis for a lawsuit.) This is, needless to say, a bad thing. So you owe it to yourself, your customers, and the insurance provider to understand the nuts and bolts of the job. That's what I want to talk about in this book.

Now, the standard disclaimer: **I am not a lawyer.** Nothing in this book is legal advice. Everything in this book consists of guidelines that I've learned in my years of handling claims. I may occasionally quote legal language, but **this is not in any way intended to carry any legal authority whatsoever.** Also, note that state and federal laws are subject to change and therefore the details may be different over time.

Now that we've gotten that out of the way, here is

the plan for this book. You are going to learn about how customer service in claims works, how contracts work (the auto policy), how to determine liability, the typical claims process, and the settlement of simple claims. We will also hit upon a few other things as we go forward.

Best of luck.

I've tried, for the most part, to speak generically with regard to claims handling, as the principles are more or less the same whether one is in Alaska or Texas or California. Now and then I will cite specifics if it's necessary to help understanding. Also, I've tried to keep it simple for the most part, and break down the parts of the job to help you get a good handle on being a claims adjuster. In addition, there will be a few stories here and there to keep things lively, because there are some frankly boring aspects of learning how to work claims. You gotta learn it, though, because it will make your job a lot easier. Seriously.

WHAT IS A CLAIMS ADJUSTER?

Why do they call claims adjusters "claims adjusters"? What is the *adjustment* part mean?

In the field of auto insurance, the reason you are a "claims adjuster" is because every claim is different. Every auto accident is different, with different factors involved. Although the processes of handling claims are often standardized, and we apply the same standards of fairness to everyone we assist during a claim, there will often be individual specifics that have to be handled, well, *specifically*.

As a claims adjuster, you are tasked with **making decisions**. Some people love this part of the job.

Some people don't. I've had folks who want to have a big guidebook of every possible specific event, in which they can consult the guidebook and figure out what to do. There is no such guidebook. (Not even this one.) That's because we are dealing with the infinite possibilities of human behavior. (If you want to hear some crazy stories, ask an adjuster who has been handling claims for a while. They'll have a few.) If you end up doing the job, you will too someday.

If you don't like making decisions, this is not the job for you.

If you don't like telling people things they don't want to hear, this is also not the job for you.

No one who speaks to you for the first time on an auto claim will be happy. The reason they are having to speak with you is they just had a car accident. Even if they're not at fault, they are still often in a state of panic. *What's gonna happen with my car? Did the other guy have insurance? Jesus, my neck is starting to hurt...do I have whiplash? The cops took my car, I have no idea where they took it – do you know where they took it? Can I get a rental? How long is this gonna take? Do I have to pay anything? Are you gonna take care of everything for me? This lawyer called me, should I call her back? And how did they know I had a car accident anyway!?! You guys are going to screw me, I know it, insurance companies screw everybody…I hope my car isn't a total loss. Jesus, WHAT IF MY CAR IS A TOTAL LOSS!?!*

Dealing with that is your job. And a few other things. But it's OK. Because you are going to learn how to deal with that.

If you're considering a career as a casualty auto adjuster, let me first tell you a couple of things. Because this is not for everybody. You have to develop a formidable set of skills in order to do well in this gig. Here's a few things you need to be able to do:

1. Read and understand some pretty dry contract language.
2. Multitask in an environment which is often hostile. You can do everything right for the rest of your career in this job and there's still going to be times you get yelled at.

3. Use "soft skills" to manage and work with people, whether in person or on the phone.
4. Find solutions in and out of the box – hence the term "adjuster."
5. Negotiate with claimants, auto body shops, and lawyers.

At one of the places I worked, I would train classes of 25 or 30 people at a time for about a two-month course. These were folks who had zero experience and then eight to twelve weeks later they would be answering calls and handling claims. The director of the training department joked that we should show the opening landing sequence of the film *Saving Private Ryan* at the beginning of the course. The message being, **not everyone will make it**. We never did that, of course, but it was a recognition that being an adjuster is demanding in many different ways. And it's not for everybody.

Being an adjuster also makes you more aware of the dangerous side of any activity. Do it for a couple of decades or more, and you'll end up viewing all events through a claims adjuster lens. Your friend will put in a swimming pool, and you'll be thinking about how much children like to drown in those things. Your auntie gets a dog, and you'll think about that one claim where the dog bit a kid's arm off and forced his mother to stab the thing to death with scissors before she called 911.

Or maybe that's just me.

If you begin to handle claims where mayhem was happened – total fires with people in the cars, multiple-fatality van wrecks – you will start to pay attention a little more when you drive. You may reach for your phone a little less. You may look in your mirrors a little more often. Just saying.

UNDERSTANDING INSURANCE

Most of you reading this book either own a car or drive a car pretty regularly. And that means you've at one time or another bought an insurance policy for it. And of course, as soon as you bought the policy, you took it home and read it cover to cover.

Just kidding. Nobody reads their insurance policy. But guess what? You should. And while you may not grow it to love policy language like I do – you should know right now I am a very sick man – you should grow to appreciate its importance. Because misunderstanding the policy contract is the source for most of the problems people have with insurance companies, and it can also cause major headaches for you. So get ready, because we are going to take a look at a typical policy in this chapter.

But first, let's talk about insurance in general for a minute. What is insurance, anyway? Why do we have insurance? We know we have to pay it every month or we might get a ticket from a police officer if they pull us over, but why do we need insurance in the first place?

I've had people describe insurance to me as a "protection racket." This is something that you might know from *The Sopranos* or a Martin Scorcese picture. Guy owns a store on a city block, gets visited by some gangsters. It's a dangerous neighborhood, they tell him. Bad things can happen. The gangsters offer their protection; in exchange, the storeowner pays a fee to the gangsters. If the storeowner refuses to pay, bad things start to happen. Maybe vandalism. Maybe a break-in or two. Or maybe there's a fire.

Insurance is not exactly like a protection racket. The main difference is that if you don't pay your premium, the insurance company won't send somebody over to break your kneecaps. Also, they aren't looking to *cause* calamities. In fact, they would very much prefer it if you don't have any incidents at all.

The reason why is that all insurance products **are essentially a bet.** A bet that the money they take in as **premium** (that is, payment for insurance coverage) will be greater than the money they pay out (in payment for claims). An insurance company has a pool of money, taken from the **earned premium** they've taken in from all their customers, and if they bet wisely, the number of claims will not result in payments that exceed the amount of money in the pool. An insurance pool works when the people who *don't* have accidents pay into the pool to cover the people who *do*.

That means anyone who wants to have an insurance company has to be good at assessing risk.

What is risk? It's a chance, or probability, of a negative outcome (among all possible outcomes). What insurance companies have to do is called **risk assessment**. The risk assessment part of an insurance company is called **underwriting**.

You do underwriting (risk assessment) all the time, by the way.

Let's say your neighbor knocks on your door and wants to borrow your lawnmower. In your head, you have to assess the risk of lending him your lawnmower. You'll think about your relationship: how well do you know this person? You'll think about their proximity: how close do they live to you? You'll think about your history: what has happened in the past when you've loaned them things? You might ask what he wants to use it for. Does he want to mow his lawn, or use parts from it to build a rocket engine in his garage? Wait, is this the guy who sells meth? And you will say yes or no depending on all those factors and more.

Your skills at risk assessment start out terrible and (hopefully) improve with age, education, and experience. Does your six-year-old want to ride on the Harley with Uncle Dave? HELLS YEAH! Bad risk assessment. A six-year-old can't always reasonably assess danger when presented with something super exciting. Or a candy bar.

Cut to ten years later. What happens when a sixteen-year-old boy is asked by his friends to take Mom's car out for a trip to Tijuana? He says YES, more often than not. Have you ever noticed that the people who die bungee jumping, or flying a wingsuit, or doing other pointless thrilling things tend to be young? Sure. Most middle-aged people don't suddenly decide to start jumping out of airplanes. Middle-aged people content themselves by buying a nice car or sleeping with someone they shouldn't. Those may be bad decisions, but they don't usually result in immediate death. Risk assessment, all things being equal, improves with age and experience. That's why young folks are so expensive to insure.

A forty-year-old person starts to remember how bad a hangover feels when you ask them to go out drinking. And they also remember they're not 26 anymore. They might still make a bad decision, but they are drawing on a better, larger pool of information.

That process of calculation is your personal risk assessment.

WHY DO WE HAVE INSURANCE AT ALL?

The reason we have insurance is that it's good for society. Really. Let's think about this for a minute.

The most dangerous thing you do every day of your life is get into a personal automobile and drive somewhere. Almost everybody knows someone who has had their lives ended or irrevocably changed by an auto accident. It's not something we like to think about it, but it's true.

A typical sedan weighs about two tons, is powered by an internal combustion engine that you fill with gasoline, can exceed speeds of 100MPH, and can be legally driven by teenagers. That is plainly nuts, but we all accept it as normal.

It's also true that an automobile can do catastrophic levels of mayhem. In June 2016, a man drove a truck into a crowd of bicyclists, killing five of them. One wrong turn, one moment of inattention, and boom.

When I was in high school and my first couple years of college, I fronted a rock band. Had a great time, played parties and bars, that sort of thing. We had a friend who was the "manager" of the band, which meant he let us practice at his house and scored us beer. A good egg. Anyway, one night he got too drunk to drive home so we made him allow his girlfriend to drive him home. Except somewhere during the journey he demanded she allow him to drive. He went into a ditch and broke his neck.

Almost everyone knows someone like that. Or has a story about an accident they were involved in when they were young. When I was a teenager we used to smoke a bowl, then take out my buddy's Firebird, and he would do donuts while I filmed the excitement hanging out the passenger window. If I'd fallen out I wouldn't be here.

Anyway, you get it. Vehicles are dangerous as hell.

In addition to these considerations, cars are also a commodity, like a home, often purchased via a payment plan. You put some percentage of the car's value down, and then continue paying it off on a monthly basis. This method of payment is necessary because most ordinary people do not have thousands of dollars available to buy automobiles outright. This **adds** to the assessment of risk. (Incidentally, your credit rating, good or bad, can affect the price of the insurance you buy. Bad credit means bad risk.)

If we put these two things together – cars are incredibly dangerous, and most people cannot come up with the money to pay for them, and it starts to become clear why insurance might be a good idea.

If nobody had auto insurance, people would go bankrupt far more often than they already do as a result of car accidents. You will find, as an adjuster, that **ordinary people are terrible judges of how expensive car accidents are**. They always think that car repairs are going to be less than they actually are. Every now and then you might have an insured that backs into somebody's parked car or has a minor incident and says, "Hey, I'm just reporting the claim, but I want to handle it myself. I'll pay for it."

This is a really bad idea.

What inevitably happens is that they tell the other person to get an estimate and the estimate comes back at $3,000 and then they call you and say "This guy is trying to rip me off! I barely touched that car!" And maybe it's a rip off but in all likelihood it isn't, because repairing automobiles is expensive. And what happens when the car goes into the shop?

Are they going to pay for a rental car for the other person? Most people will not have the thousands of dollars in damages they might cause by making a mistake on the road.

Which is why you have insurance. All insurance is designed to protect personal property of some kind. In the case of a house, the idea is that you will be covered for certain types of accidental disasters (usually called **perils**) like water leaks, for example. There is also coverage for things like theft of contents.

THE POLICY CONTRACT

If you've ever purchased insurance for your car, then you have received a contract. It gets sent to you by the insurance company and you promptly put it away and never look at it again.

Well, you're gonna need to look at it. We need to understand this document in order to do the job of an adjuster.

As an example, I am going to be drawing from the **Texas** contract throughout this book. However, I will be alluding to other states at various times for contrast purposes. There are many advantages to using Texas as the base, including the fact that a Texas license is *reciprocal* to many other states. What that means is that if you have a Texas license, there are many states that will allow you to work claims in that state if you are licensed in Texas. Note that this does **not** mean you are automatically issued a license in that particular state.

So, for example, if you are issued a Texas license, all things being equal, you should be able to handle claims in California, Alabama, and many other states. You would not, however, be able to handle claims in New Jersey, Oklahoma, or several other states without obtaining their specific licenses. Always remember that It depends on the specific state regulations. Also note that these are subject to change by the legislatures of these states.

Now that we've gotten that out of the way, let's look at the Texas policy.

It used to be, many years ago, that all Texas policies were the same. That policy was called the TPAP (the Texas Personal Auto Policy) and you may hear older folks like me still refer to it that way. However, that is no longer the case. **The**

Texas Department of Insurance (also known as TDI) now sets the regulations for all sorts of different auto and property policies. So although most of the language we will review is standard, be aware that when you start working for an insurance carrier, they will likely have a policy with different language.

PARTIES

The auto policy is a **contract**. A contract is an agreement between two or more parties that solidifies in writing what each party agrees to do for the other one. In the case of an automobile policy, this is usually referred to as the **insuring agreement**. The insuring agreement says, in effect, "we will agree to cover you in a loss as specified by the terms of the contract."

Let's say you went down to the racetrack to play the horses. You put a certain amount of money down on a horse with a certain set of odds. The racetrack says if this horse *wins, places,* or *shows,* depending on what kind of bet you put down, you win some money. That's a simple sort of contract: If X happens, you are paid; if any other result happens, you are not paid.

In theory, contracts can be either verbal or written. When you tell your kid to stop screaming in Target or else they're going to be locked in the attic for the rest of their lives, that is a *verbal contract*. You are contracting with your child to cease vocalizing on the threat of eternal imprisonment. In the world of insurance, we work with and agree to *written contracts*: that is, agreements in which the insurance company agrees to take certain actions in the event of certain events, provided payment is made.

The basic idea is that you give some money up front to the insurance carrier, or agree to make payments on a regular basis until the contract is fulfilled, and in return the insurance company promises to pay certain amounts if certain events happen for a certain length of time – typically 30 days, six months, or perhaps a year. That length of time is referred to as the coverage period. It will be shown as dates on your insurance card.

Those dates will be shown on your insurance card and/or on your **declarations page**. The declarations page, frequently called the "dec" in insurance parlance, refers to the summary sheet of all the coverages on a policy. When somebody asks for a dec page, or a dec sheet, that summary is what they mean.

If you look at your own insurance card, you might notice the two dates we are talking about. You should see the words **"effective date"** with a date attached – say, 11/22/17. You will also see the words **"expiration date"** with another date next to it – say, 5/22/18.

In this case we have a sixth-month policy. The effective date is the first date the policy was started. The expiration date is the date the policy ends. The coverage period is all of the time between those two dates, assuming payments were made and the policy never canceled. If a person has an accident on 11/18/17, then that accident would not be covered by the policy, because that is prior to the effective date of 11/22/17.

Any contract, including an auto contract, has parties. The parties to the contract are divided up into two: the **first party** and the **second party**. There is also the concept of the **third party**, which designates anyone who is not a part of the contract.

(This makes me think of the old Marx Brothers routine in which Groucho tells Chico, "The party of the first part shall be known in this contract as the party of the first part," and Chico responds, "Well that's no good, I don't like it." It's online – go look for it next time you need a break.)

The first party is the person getting the insurance. The person signing on the dotted line to obtain the insurance policy and that person's spouse. This person (plus spouse) is also called the **Named Insured**.

The second party is the insurance company what wrote the contract.

The third party is anyone who is not directly connected to the contract as a participant.

EXAMPLE

Juanita Peron just bought herself a new car. While she is at the dealership, she and the dealer call Cash Me Insurance to start a policy on the new car. When she gets this new policy, she has entered into a contractual relationship with the insurance company. With respect to this contract, Juanita is the first party and Cash Me is the second party. **Everyone else in the world is a third party with regard to the contract**.

Note: if Juanita has a **lienholder** on her vehicle, the lienholder also is considered a first party when it comes time to pay on any claims. A lienholder is anyone who is loaning Juanita money to purchase the vehicle, typically a bank or dealership. More on this later.

One very important thing to keep in mind: in general, there is an agreed-upon principle (going back to Roman contract law) that in case of ambiguity in the contract, the law will interpret it *against* the party what drew up the contract. In other words, if the language isn't clear in the contract, then courts (in general) will resolve that lack of clarity in favor of the person signing the contract. This is because the person drawing up the contract has more power than the person signing it.

You might have a question at this point. The question might go something like: *if third parties aren't part of a contract, why the heck are we talking about them?*

Good question. The reason is that we deal with third parties all the time. Let's say your insured backs into somebody's parked car. The owner of that car is a third party, and that's who we will be calling to settle out the claim. Make sense?

So that is the introductory bit on contracts. Let's look at one more concept before we move on to the next chapter.

TORTS

A **tort** is a civil wrong. A tort refers to a wrong that impedes another person's rights or creates a specific harm against another person or entity. It's not necessarily a crime. If you lend me your dog and I lose the dog accidentally, I owe you some compensation but I won't be going to prison.

A **civil court** is therefore distinct from **criminal court**. In criminal court, the state is prosecuting an individual for violations of the criminal code. A guilty finding produces fines and/or imprisonment and, occasionally, death. **In civil court, the award is always money.**

In the famous O. J. Simpson murder trial, the state

was not able to convict Simpson in a criminal trial. In a criminal trial, a unanimous verdict of the 12 jurors is required to secure the conviction. This did not happen. However, the family of Nicole Brown Simpson sued O.J. in civil court, for violations of Nicole's civil rights (in essence, that he had denied her life, liberty, and happiness, by killing her.) The civil trial resulted in a large monetary award for the family.

In the claims world, we are always talking about **money**, not punishment, although sometimes insureds don't understand that. Our world is in the civil, not criminal. It is the world of torts. As a claims adjuster, you are constantly being asked to set values in monetary terms.

Claims adjusting is generally concerned only with torts. In special cases adjusters can be involved in investigating crimes, but those folks are called SIU – a **Special Investigation Unit**. They typically handle cases where there is potential fraud.

As an adjuster, part of your job will involve looking for possible fraud indicators, and referring those cases to your SIU unit.

A quick note on fraud. Never, ever, use the word "fraud" on the phone. Never accuse anyone of being a fraud. You are not a police officer or a judge or anyone with any legal authority to be making pronouncements like that.

If you think something is questionable about a claim, what you will typically be asked to do is refer it to your SIU unit. The SIU unit will look into the matter and report back. They will handle all the investigative aspects of the case – they might get another recorded statement, for example, or in some rare cases they might get an **Examination Under Oath** (EUO). But again, that will be someone else's determination.

I used to tell my classes that I'd rather they use the other F-word than say "fraud" on the phone. Of course I don't want you to say either, but I just want to underline the seriousness of what I'm saying. We don't accuse people of any crimes, ok? Thanks for agreeing.

'

THE INSURANCE POLICY

A Texas policy is broken up into the following sections:

PART A – LIABILITY

PART B – MEDICAL COVERAGE

PART C – UNINSURED MOTORIST

PART D – PHYSICAL DAMAGE COVERAGE

PART E – DUTIES

PART F – GENERAL

We will briefly look at all of these, one at a time.

PART A - LIABILITY

The first thing your auto policy talks about is **liability, which is coverage for other people if you are at fault.** Liability is split up into **Bodily Injury** (people) and **Property Damage** (stuff).

If you are at your friend's house, and you accidentally break a glass, you would typically offer to replace it or cover the cost of getting a new one. The act of breaking the glass is a tort, what we talked about earlier. You become "liable" for breaking the object. Your replacement of the glass makes your friend "whole" again. They get a new glass.

The same thing is true of an auto accident. If you accidentally strike someone's car, the car may sustain damage and the persons inside it may be injured. Liability coverage on your auto policy will attempt to make the other person whole, up to a certain limit that you choose when buying a policy. The liability coverage is triggered by you being guilty of the tort.

Bodily Injury on your auto policy covers the injuries to any people in the other vehicle, or your own vehicle, if you are at fault in an accident. When you are at fault – that is, you are primarily responsible for the injuries to another person, Bodily Injury kicks in to cover the associated costs.

Property Damage on your auto policy covers the damages to any property not belonging to you, that is damaged as a result of your actions. This is often another car, but it could be a house, a boat, a business, or virtually any sort of personal property, including pets. (Yes, pets are considered personal property.)

That means if you run over someone's dog, the owner's love for the dog plays no role in the amount you pay. However much it costs to get a replacement dog is what you would owe. And a cat? How much does it cost to get a cat? Usually they're free. I have cats, and I love my cats, and they are special to me. But unfortunately, I would not receive much compensation if someone were to run over my cat. I would have to satisfy myself by using a baseball bat to provide moral instruction to the person who hurt my cat.

Now of course there are special dogs what have papers and yes, you would take into account. I've noticed people get very worked up about the pets angle. One of my students, who was working on the floor as a claims adjuster, interrupted my class one day so we could speak out in the hall. He was so excited because the insured had run over an old lady and her dog. "It was just like you said," he said. "The dog was a mutt." I told him I appreciated how excited he was to handle his first such claim scenario, but to please remember how the old lady would feel about the situation (she lived). Empathy is important too. (We'll get to customer service later.)

A standard Texas auto policy (as of 2017) has minimum limits in the following amounts:

Bodily Injury (abbreviated BI): $30,000/$60,000
Property Damage (abbreviated PD): $25,000

Notice the difference in how the amounts are written out. Bodily Injury is **a split limit**. Property Damage is a **single limit**.

The split refers to the fact that under BI, there is a

$30,000 *per person* limit with a $60,000 *per claim* limit.

Suppose you were in an auto accident in which three people were injured. The adjuster could pay a maximum of $30,000 to any one person, and if that happened, the other two people would be forced to accept a total up to the remaining $30,000. So you could, for example, settle the second person's claim for $20,000 and the third person's claim for $10,000, thus exhausting all the BI coverage available.

You must keep within these $30,000/$60,000 limits. You could not, for example, settle one person for $45,000, even if the other two people were willing to split the remaining $15,000. The $30,000 is a hard cap for an individual person. The $60,000 is a hard cap on the whole claim, whether you injure two people or hit a clown car and injure 17 guys. You could pay one of them $30,000 but the other 16 would have to split the remainder. And yes, things like this do happen, but settling injury claims will be another book of its own.

Under PD, there is only a single limit of $25,000. This is the total amount regardless of the amount of damaged property. So, if you were to accidentally strike one vehicle and send it careening into another vehicle and a house, they would all have to split the same $25,000. When someone has an accident that is more than the total coverage available, this is called an **excess** situation. This is bad news for the insured. You have an excess situation when an insured's personal assets are in play as the result of an accident.

Please note that so far we have been discussing **minimum limits**. You can typically get higher limits, although not from every insurance company. People need higher levels of protection if they have significant assets. Obviously, Beyonce doesn't have a 30/60 policy; assuming she even drives herself, she would carry a policy with millions of dollars in coverage.

Usually the first thing people do after learning about claims is to raise the liability limits on their own policies. After you start seeing a few hair-raising scenarios, you start to realize how low minimum limits truly are. And this is Texas – there are some states that will let you drive around with $5,000 property damage limits or $10,000/$20,000 bodily injury limits. How much does the average car cost? How much does the average hospital visit cost? Low limits are cheaper, but it is somewhat of a gamble.

PART B – MEDICAL COVERAGE

Part B of the Texas policy covers first-party medical coverage. There are two types of coverages available under Part B. The first is called **Medical Payments** (MP). The second is called **Personal Injury Protection** (PIP). These are usually referred to as Part B1 (MP) and Part B2 (PIP).

Texas is unusual in offering both Medical Payments coverage and Personal Injury Protection. Most states offer one or the other.

Medical Payments coverage is for injuries to people in the insured vehicle, including the driver. It is designed to reimburse for direct medical expenses and funeral expenses from injuries incurred in an auto accident.

Personal Injury Protection coverage is also for those in the insured's vehicle, including the driver. However, it can also cover 80% of wage loss (if a person misses work due to injury), personal services if the person doesn't work (i.e., someone to wash clothes, mow the lawn, and the like), and funeral expenses.

Both MP and PIP are single limits. The minimum is typically $1000 for MP and $2500 for PIP, but you can get much more than this, up to a million or more depending on the insurer. Insurers will often have customers pick one of the two coverages rather than have both.

There is one other important different between MP and PIP which has to do with **subrogation**. Subrogation means that payments under that coverage can be recovered for someone else. We will talk more about subrogation later, but for the moment let's just note that **MP is subrogable**, and **PIP is not subrogable**.

PART C –UNINSURED MOTORIST COVERAGE

Uninsured Motorist/Underinsured Motorist (UM/UIM) coverage is the most complex of all the coverages on an auto policy, and also the most dangerous for companies to handle, as it easy to make a mistake that lands them in hot water. The idea behind Uninsured/Underinsured Motorist is to assist in situations where a third party is at-fault for an accident but they don't have any insurance or they have insufficient insurance. Those situations can be broken down like so:

1. You are in your vehicle stopped at a stop light when you are suddenly struck from behind by a third-party automobile. Before you have a chance to recover from the accident, the car speeds off. You have no information about the person or vehicle that hit you.

2. The same incident occurs, but the person gets out of their car and takes responsibility for the accident. Unfortunately, the person does not carry valid insurance.

3. The same incident occurs, but the person has a minimum Texas liability of $25,000. Your vehicle is totaled and is worth $30,000. The at-fault third party is **underinsured**. In other words, they don't have enough to coverage to make you whole with regard with your vehicle.

Uninsured/Underinsured Motorist insurance tends to be complicated. For now, these are just the basic details. Also note, that under the UMPD coverage in Texas, there is a $250 deductible. Other states have different rules, and some states don't have Uninsured coverage at all.

PART D – PHYSICAL DAMAGE COVERAGE

Physical Damage coverage is typically split into two categories: **Collision** (often abbreviated CL), and **Comprehensive** (or Other than Collision, often abbreviated Comp or OC). It is a no-fault coverage – that means, in this context, that you can use your collision or comprehensive coverage whether you're at fault or not.

This coverage is for damage to your car and carries a **deductible**. A deductible is an amount that you responsible for before the insurance kicks in – sometimes referred to as the self-insured portion. If your deductible is $500, that means the policy will pay for any and all related damages over $500.

Unlike most medical deductibles in health insurance, you don't pay one deductible to cover the whole year. **Every incident requires a separate deductible**. In other words, you can't get hailed on in March, get into a fender bender in

July, back into your garage in November and then call the insurance company and say "OK, I'm ready to make a claim now." (And yes, people try this.) You have three separate claims with three separate deductibles.

Collision coverage is designed to handle incidents in which the insured vehicle strikes a physical object with the automobile. This is often another vehicle, but could also include a rock, a house, a guardrail, a tree, or any other sort of physical property.

Comprehensive is designed to handle incidents in which the insured vehicle is damaged by something other than an actual collision with an object. Most policies name a series of perils – bad things that might happen – but these are just common perils and it's not meant to be exclusive.

Some examples of comprehensive losses:

- Fire, whether it originates in the vehicle or from an external source

- Partial or Total Theft; a partial theft is when a vehicle gets broken into because someone wants something inside the vehicle, such as a stereo, whereas a Total Theft refers to the entire vehicle being stolen

- Missiles can be either thrown, launched, or dropped onto the vehicle; this would include a baseball hit into a car windshield, or an object flying off the back of a truck

- Earthquake or natural disasters, like wind/hail or flooding

- Vandalism of all kinds

- Glass breakage, as in rock chips and the like

- Riot, short of insurrection

- Animal or birdstrike; for purposes of this coverage, humans are usually considered animals

Yeah, that last part is true. Drive into a bear, it's comprehensive; drive into your Aunt Edna, it's still comprehensive.

DEDUCTIBLES

Comprehensive and Collision claims have a

deductible attached. These can be $250, $500, $1,000, $1,250 or other amounts, depending on the insurance company. The basic idea behind a deductible is that there is a *self-insured* portion. The customer purchases OC or CL coverage with the knowledge that if there is a loss, the first money will come out of the insured's pocket. So that if a person has a $250 deductible has a loss worth $1,000, the insurance company will cover $750.

And remember, the deductible refreshes with each new loss. That also applies to an incident in which the insured hits her own car. (Yes, that happens fairly often actually.) Let's say a married couple has two cars, and they are both on one auto policy with $500 deductibles. Now imagine that the husband accidentally backs his car into the one belonging to his wife. Ouch! They are out $1000. Each of those incidents is *separate* and will require a *separate* deductible. They don't like hearing that, but it's how it is.

Very often, when there is a minor crack in the windshield (dime-sized with no spreading), an insured can get that fixed with no deductible. Windshield *replacement*, however, will always carry a deductible. The loss will be covered under

Comprehensive coverage.

PARTS E & F

Part E – DUTIES AFTER AN ACCIDENT

This section deals with the duties the insured has to the company. For example, an insured typically has the duty to report accidents and incidents in a timely fashion. If the insured has an accident and takes a year to report it, there may not be coverage because of the lapse of time.

Now this isn't as simple as it looks, because in most cases the standard qualifier is that the late reporting has to interfere with the insurance company's investigation. A delay of days, weeks, or even months often won't have much effect on the investigation, unless there is no police report or there are some other details in dispute. As with all things, in cases like this the circumstances will vary. However, in all such cases we will send a **Reservation of Rights** letter. The Reservation of Rights letter is a letter sent to the insured to warn them they may not have coverage for a particular loss for a particular reason.

Part F – GENERAL PROVISIONS

Part F usually is a grab-bag of items that don't fit in other parts of the policy. One thing that is typically addressed is where the policy is effective. Auto policies will typically cover losses anywhere in the United States and its territories, like Puerto Rico. Policies will often also cover losses in Canada. However, Mexico and Europe do not ordinarily count as territories for the purpose of the policy. Let me repeat: YOUR AMERICAN INSURANCE DOES NOT COVER YOU IN MEXICO. If you take away one thing from this section, it should be, for the love of God, to BUY MEXICAN INSURANCE BEFORE YOU GO INTO MEXICO. Do NOT rely on your insurance policy.

Have you seen the movie *Blood In, Blood Out?* First of all, if you haven't, go see that movie. Second of all, if you have, you know what the hell I'm talking about.

The last place you need an insurance lesson is in a Mexican jail. This book will not help you.

Keep in mind that these are general definitions and terms for the purpose of discussion. Specific policies always differ from each other, not only within a state but from state to state. California policies look completely different from Michigan policies, which look completely different from policies in Massachusetts. But we've got to start somewhere.

ENDORSEMENTS

Policy **endorsements are usually defined as additions to a standard auto policy**, although some insurance companies refer to any change done to a policy as an endorsement. It varies. For our discussion here, I will treat an endorsement as an addition to insurance.

An example of an endorsement is rental car coverage. This coverage is called **rental reimbursement**. Please note the actual terms used. As a matter of customer service, insurance companies will often set up a direct bill with an insurance company to pay as the rental is incurred. However, *they don't have to by contract.* Technically they could have the customer incur the rental costs, then be reimbursed by the insurance company, just like it says.

What is owed under rental reimbursement? The coverage will have a daily limit and a 30-day limit in most cases, although policies differ. So rental coverage might be $20 a day up to a $600 maximum, or $30 a day up to a $900 maximum, and so on depending on what the company offers. Sometimes they just cover an amount equal to whatever type of vehicle is insured under the policy.

Also note that the auto policy stipulates that a rental vehicle is provided in the event of an accident and for the length of time required to repair the car to its former condition. Rentals cannot be obtained when your car is in the shop for a mechanical issue, or just because you want to drive out to Long Island for the weekend. Also, rentals aren't automatically for 30-day periods or until the full amount covered is gone. If your car needs to be in the shop for two weeks, your rental lasts for two weeks.

This all might seem like common sense, but believe me you will get people who believe otherwise.

Another endorsement often offered is **Towing & Labor** or **Roadside Assistance**. This will pay for a certain amount for a mechanical problem with the insured car. It's usually for a tow or for someone to come out to charge the battery or change a tire. This has to be from some sort of mechanical breakdown.

Keep in mind that a tow made in the course of an accident is not normally covered under Towing & Labor. It is part of the Collision or Comprehensive loss and paid out of that coverage. As always, however, check your policy for more details.

WHAT IS A LOSS?

In claims, we talk about **losses**. When a person makes a claim, it's because they have had some type of loss. The first thing an adjuster has to do is determine whether an actual loss has been suffered, and whether that loss is covered. The coverage question is the most important question that needs to be answered at the beginning of the claim.

BASIC COVERAGE QUESTIONS

For an auto claim, we need to know that (1) the insurance policy is active, (2) the vehicle is listed on the policy, and (3) the loss is within the scope of the policy. We will also need to determine if there are any potential coverage issues, but the more complex coverage questions we will cover later. For now, let's look at these three things.

First: is the insurance policy active? A person buys an insurance policy for a particular **term**. That is, the coverage begins at a certain date and time, and it ends (or renews) at a certain date and time. Let's say you buy an insurance policy that begins April 1, 2018. Obviously, if you have an accident on March 20, 2018, there is no coverage because you hadn't purchased the policy yet. Makes sense, no?

Second: is the vehicle listed on the policy? An insurance policy (for a private individual) is bought for a specific car which is identified by a VIN – vehicle identification number. The policy will list a 2015 Hyundai Eleantra Touring, for example, and it will have the VIN listed. This is the car on the policy. If an insured calls in a loss on a 2012 Ford Ranger, and the Ranger is not listed on the policy, then we have a coverage issue. That doesn't necessarily mean there is no coverage, but we will have to do some more investigation to determine what will happen in a claim.

Third: A loss must be sudden and accidental. It cannot be "wear and tear," that is, happening through natural deterioration over time.

Things that don't count as a "loss" for purposes of the insurance contract:

- Any sort of mechanical breakdown.
- Anything that results from maintenance. If you don't put oil in your car, eventually your engine will be destroyed. You cannot make a claim for this, because it isn't

sudden and accidental. You know you have to put oil in a car.

- Deliberately damaging your car, like if you drove into a lake on purpose. This is called an intentional act.

- Anything that isn't generally "sudden and accidental." So if you leave your car out under a tree for six months, birds poop on it and destroy the paint, that doesn't count. The damage was accrued over a long period of time. If a squirrel eats the engine because you parked it near a farm or something, that probably would be covered. (That may sound crazy, but I've had claims where rodents ate up tubing or other parts of an engine.)

This is just the beginning. What you need to get used to is asking these questions right from the start of every claim you handle. Do we even have a policy? Sometimes claims get called in but our supposed insured doesn't have a policy with us, or they did two years ago but haven't had one since. In fact, sometimes insurance companies get sued on the basis of very little information. Suppose someone gets rear-ended, and the other guy drives off. The only thing the claimant knows is that the hit-and-run driver had a particular insurance company sticker on the back of the vehicle, so they sue the insurance company. (Again, sounds nuts, but I've seen it happen.)

THE POLICY DOES NOT COVER EVERYTHING

The aspect that customers, or insureds, often get confused on is the idea that they bought an insurance policy for their car, and therefore the insurance company should be able to handle everything about a loss. Many complaints are generated simply because the person who bought the policy never read it or did not understand what is covered or not covered.

People tend to think that insurance companies are ought to get them. However, the reality is that all contracts – whether you are buying a house or a car or getting married – do not *cover everything*. That isn't realistic. The contract has terms and conditions like any other contract.

As an adjuster, it becomes your responsibility to accurately and clearly explain how the contract works. Often, that means being the bearer of bad news.

Incidentally, this is also why you should never use the term "full coverage." **There is no such thing as "full coverage."** What it is typically used to mean is a car that has Comprehensive and Collision coverage, but to someone who is not an expert it implies much more than it could ever possibly mean. You can't buy insurance that allows you to set your own car on fire like the Joker and then expect the insurance company to pay your claim, right? Of course not. There are limits to everything. So never say "full coverage" to anyone.

As noted before, a loss is a one-time event. You don't get to collect a little damage here, and a little damage there, and now it hailed so let's take care of all of it for one deductible. Those are separate incidents.

The same thing applies to repairs. Let's say the insured had parked their car in a store lot and had it backed into by an unknown vehicle that drove off. The insured makes a claim, pays the deductible, and the insurance company handles the claim. Everything gets handled the way it should.

The insured gets the car back from the shop, but now there is a new problem. The door, freshly repaired by the shop, has a shine on the paint that makes it slightly different from the rest of the paint on the car. Shops these days have excellent blending techniques, but it is not always possible to get a perfect 100% match with the rest of the car.

The insured proposes a solution: Paint the whole car. Since the accident caused the damaged door, and the door doesn't match the rest of the car, surely that's the only thing that makes sense to do. That sounds reasonable, doesn't it?

Well, let's think about it for a moment. The new, fresh paint doesn't match with the rest of the car. We need to ask a key question: *Why doesn't the paint match?*

The answer is simple. Because the paint on the rest of the car has faded away over time a little bit. And why has it faded away over time? Because that's what everything does in this universe. Over time. Which is another way of saying **wear and tear**.

Is wear and tear a covered loss? No, by the terms of the contract.

And that is why insurance companies will not re-paint your entire car after you've had an accident (unless it's warranted by the accident itself). If insurance companies had to re-paint whole cars every time somebody had a fender bender, body shops would be very happy and your insurance premiums would be more astronomical than they already are.

Most of the "rules" for insurance claims are set in just to make sure everybody is playing on a level field. And many of these rules have been put in place as the result of court cases over time.

COVERED VEHICLES

Of course, the first thing to look for on an auto accident, as we noted, is to check if the car is on the insurance policy.

If it isn't, that doesn't necessarily mean we have no coverage, because an insurance policy will usually cover a driver in a **temporary substitute vehicle**.

A temporary substitute vehicle is exactly that – a vehicle that you're using to get around while your primary vehicle is in the shop or not available for some reason. You borrowed your neighbor's car to get some groceries. You are driving a loaner while your car is getting some mechanical work done. You had to driver your sister's Dodge pickup because she left it in a parking lot after going on a drunk. That sort of thing.

There are limitations on how this extends. First of all, it has to be an ordinary vehicle designed for use on public roads and bearing a certain weight. A go-cart, a motorized wheelchair, a motorcycle (those require special policies usually), a tractor-trailer (ditto), an armored tank, a cherry-picker, etc. are not "vehicles" for an auto policy. It has to be a normal car or truck or van or something commonly used on public roads. If you're not sure about whether your policy covers the particular vehicle you are thinking of using, talk to your insurance company.

Second, this cannot be a vehicle furnished and available for your regular use. If there is a vehicle commonly parked at your house that belongs to someone who lives with you – friend, cousin, or whatever the situation is – that vehicle will **typically not be covered if you drive it.**

Why not?

Sometimes folks have a hard time with this at first, so let's go through an example. Imagine you live alone with your car, and your brother needs to crash with you for a year while he finishes school. He has his own car. One day you borrow it to make a beer run and have an accident. Your brother calls the insurance company to make a claim and they ask how long he's been living at the residence, and he says "six months."

They will probably not cover the loss. Because if the insurance company agrees to cover the accident, they have been **providing free insurance for your brother.**

When an insurance company agrees to take on your vehicle for a policy, they recognize there are certain risks that come from doing so. That's why your driving records matters to your policy premium. That's why your credit rating can sometimes affect the premium. There are other factors, such as where you live – on the average, cities are more costly than rural areas (because population density affects accident and theft rates).

However, if your brother is living with you, and you can generally access his car any time you want, with the idea that insurance will cover any losses that involve you as a driver, they are providing free insurance. That free insurance comes without the insurance company *knowing what sort of a risk they're covering.*

Basically, when this situation comes up, as an adjuster you will need to carefully check the policy to see what the conditions are, and also do a careful investigation to determine the circumstances. Again, I'm not saying there will be no coverage, but just that we have a coverage issue and need to investigate the situation further.

While we are on the subject, let me say one another thing. You will notice that I am careful to always say things like "sometimes," "usually," or "typically," and so on. **That's because there are very few absolutes in claims handling. That's why you're called a claims adjuster**. It's not because you are adjusting in favor of one person or another. It's because life is complicated and it's impossible to set black-and-white rules for every possible situation.

If you're the sort of person who wants to a guide to your actions so you can follow it like the Ten Commandments, you will not like claims adjusting. You will have guidelines, and the law, and rules of ethics, but you will not have a perfect "if-then" set of rules for every situation. You will have to think, and use your common sense and your judgment, and eventually your own experience. Being a good adjuster means continually weighing, thinking, and applying what you know.

Okay, end of aside.

COVERED PEOPLE

So who is covered by your insurance policy?

It depends.

First and foremost, the **Named Insured (NI)** is covered by an insurance policy. That will be, as we discussed, the person who signed on the line that is dotted to obtain the policy, as well as the spouse if there is one.

Any children are also covered as "family

members," but they are considered the Named Insured. (This can be an important distinction because you are only allowed, in most cases, to discuss the policy with the NI. The children don't count – unless they get a power of attorney. This can come up if the NI becomes infirm or is injured for some reason.)

In addition, most insurance policies are written to be "omnibus policies." It used to be common for insurance contracts to only specifically insure the person who bought the policy while excluding everyone else. Since it's pretty common to loan your car to a buddy for a short time, and most people think that is reasonable, this turned out to be **bad public policy**. Because handling insurance policies this way greatly increases the number of uninsured drivers, and therefore defeats the purpose of requiring insurance in the first place.

What that means is that, generally speaking, it's OK for other people to drive your car with your permission. Of course there are always exceptions, but that is the general rule.

However, what constitutes "permissive use" may surprise you. **Permissive use does not have to be**

explicit. It can be *implied*, and implied permission can be as basic as leaving the keys out in a visible area while the other person is at your house. In other words, if you are having a party, and your keys are out on the table, and someone you don't know uses your car and wrecks it, there is probably implied permission.

Let's take another scenario. What if your kid is using the car with your permission, but he gets blackout drunk and passes out in the backseat, and his buddy drives to make a meth score and ends up in an accident? Is there implied permission?

Well, let's think about the situation. Did you give your son permission? Yes. Did your son then extend permission to his friend? No, he was out. Does the buddy think he has permission to use the vehicle while your son is blacked out in the backseat?

Probably.

In the example I just gave, the driver died in the accident and the son was in a coma, while the Named Insured was out of the country and unreachable. We were in limbo for a while and required a lot of investigation, but it was always likely that permissive use would extend.

In fact, if you are ever pondering why a certain rule is the way it is in claims handling, often it's because it went to court at some point. Not always, but often somebody died or was severely maimed and the stakes were sufficiently high enough to go to court and determine whether or not something was covered.

Permissive use can be complicated. Make no assumptions until you've done your investigation.

In general, the policy is interpreted liberally with regard to drivers. It does not extend to thieves, but most other people, unless they have a Named Driver Exclusion.

NAMED DRIVER EXCLUSION (NDE)

Let's say you are a mom and your adult son lives with you. Your son has a couple of DWIs on his record and his living with you and using your car is going to send your rates through the roof. So you decide to tell your son to never use your car and agree to a **Named Driver Exclusion** for him. The insurance company agrees not to charge you for the son and you agree that if he does, the insurance company will bear no responsibility.

That's an NDE. **And it means that no coverage applies, period.** No liability (if you remember, coverage for other people) and no physical damage (coverage for the car he is driving). None. Without exception. Because you signed that form and that is the agreement.

Of course, there are exceptions for certain states. For example, Nevada doesn't like NDEs so even if you get one, it only applies to physical damage. Nevada says everybody has to have minimum liability limits, no exceptions. And it's their ballgame so they have the right to set the rules.

Just to extend that point, an insurance contract cannot refute or fail to maintain the standards imposed by the state it is written in. To do otherwise would mean the contract is illegal. That should make sense by now. The state (and its courts) is the ultimate arbiter of what goes on in terms of insurance. In Texas, that would be TDI (the Texas Department of Insurance).

Talking about exclusions, there are several standard ones that tend to be policy contracts, and they are mostly common sense. There is often a felony exclusion – that is, if you are using the car to commit a crime, there is no coverage if you have an accident. There is also typically a "fleeing from the police" exclusion – that should make sense to everybody. Racing is typically (but not always) excluded from coverage. If you damage your car doing anything shown in *The Fast and the Furious* films, there will normally not be insurance coverage for that.

SUMMING UP

A loss must be instantaneous and accidental, and a covered vehicle is a either listed on the policy or a temporary substitute, and a covered person is either a Named Insured, a family member, or someone driving with permission.

More or less. In most ordinary cases.

But there are always things that come up . For example, how about you live in Texas but your kid goes to school at USC? Is she covered while living in Southern California? Well…yes, usually, if you are still paying some of her bills, claiming her on taxes, and she comes home during the summer and that sort of thing. When she gets her own place and becomes an independent person, she will need to get her own policy. When is that moment? Who knows, right? It depends, like everything else. But those are some of the considerations.

STATUTES OF LIMITATION

One other thing to keep in consideration for claims is that they have a Statute of Limitation. This varies widely depending on what state you are working in. Since we've been using Texas as an example, we'll stay there. The SOL for both Bodily Injury and Property Damage claims in Texas is 2 years. That means, from the date of the accident, the claimant has 2 years to resolve the situation before they lose the legal right to sue. That's what an SOL is realty measuring – the ability to sue for damages. For the insured, this is typically longer, and indeed in Texas contract SOL is 4 years. However, it is not 4 years from the date of accident but from the date of the breach of contract.

For standard auto non-injury claims, typically you will only need to worry about the SOL for Property

Damage. On the vast majority of your claims, you won't have to worry about it at all, because you are going to turn and burn these claims and get them paid and out the door. If you're handling property damage exclusively and you're having to frequently worry about the Statutes of Limitation, you are doing it wrong. The idea is to investigate coverage and liability promptly and get the insureds and claimants taken care of as efficiently as possible.

INVESTIGATION: THE RECORDED STATEMENT

Whenever a new claim is received, that claim is passed on to an adjuster who will then commence an investigation. As we discussed, the first thing to figure out is coverage. For that, we get the details of the loss (what happened in the accident) and combine that with the coverage factors that we discussed in the last chapter. Is the car listed on the policy? Is the driver listed on the policy? Did the accident occur within the policy term (i.e., the dates that the policy is in effect)? Is the policy paid?

THE ACCIDENT INVESTIGATION

Once the basic loss details have been recorded –

sometimes by a Reporting group or sometimes by the adjuster, depending on how the claims organization is structured – it's time to get a **recorded statement**.

The process is really quite simple. What you will be doing is getting the basic facts of loss from all of the involved parties in an accident or loss. Depending on the type of loss, a recorded statement can be done in anytime between 5 and 25 minutes. More complex losses (theft, worker's compensation, complex liability) can extend the statement to an hour or more.

Whenever I take a recorded statement I explain to the person exactly what I am doing. I also give examples of some of the information I will be requesting, so if they need to get the driver's license out or something else they can do before we start recording.

The next thing I will do is say something like "Let me explain how this works. I am going to go through a series of questions to set up your information, and then the basic accident details, and then I will ask you to explain what happened in your words. I just need to get the questions answered first to make sure I understand all the details of your story." Because people want to give their stories, and you want to let them know there will be a little delay before they can go. You have to impose that slight bit of structure on them so you can effectively get everything they say down.

Once I've given them an idea of what I'm doing, I start the recording.

ARE RECORDED STATEMENTS REQUIRED?

What if the person doesn't want to give a recorded statement? Lawyers on television are always telling people not to cooperate with the insurance company and never give a statement. The reality is we can't force people to give statements. I mean, this isn't the Spanish Inquisition. (Because nobody expects the…aw, you know.)

Although having said that, our contract with the insureds actually does compel their cooperation. If they fail to give us a statement, by the letter of the policy they are endangering their coverage. Do we really want to go there? Not really. Do we want to even mention it? Not unless there is some sort of an extreme situation. Guy doesn't want to give a statement on a deer claim, don't start World War III. Instead, try to find out what the objection is. *Try to find the why.* And then you can explain to the insured why it's a good idea to provide a statement, and all we're trying to do is establish the facts of the case. Which is true.

If a third party doesn't want to give a statement, she doesn't have to. They don't have contractual obligations. However, you can point out that you are, once again, just trying to establish the facts and resolve the claim. And in order to investigate the claim, you need to get statements from all relevant parties to establish what happened.

Incidentally, supposing your driver is a minor (below the legal age of adulthood). If you know either an insured or a claimant is a minor, you must have a parent OK the recorded statement. Easiest way to do this is just have them join in on the statement and confirm that they agree to allow the statement. You just have to remind them that after that point, you will expect the minor to answer all the questions. Some helicopter parents will start telling you what happened in the accident when they weren't even present.

Another question: Are written statements acceptable substitutes for oral recorded statements? In some cases, yes, although a recorded interview is always preferred. Sometimes it comes down to necessity or preference on behalf of the claimant or insured. In general, a written statement is better than nothing.

In the old days, in preparing for a statement I would have also gotten a scratch piece of paper, ready to draw a picture. I still think that after speaking with a person, if you can't draw out the accident on a piece of paper then you don't understand what happened. It's just incredibly useful. It used to be (in the days when we used mini-cassette recorders…I know, I'm old) that we also had sheets we would staple the recorders to, which was nice because you could tell at a glance which claim it was. Because of the picture you drew. Anyway, it is usually impractical these days to do it, but if you get a chance I recommend it. It really helps you clear things up.

INTRO

Your introduction should be simple – depending on the carrier, it will be something like, "It is August

22, 2017, and the time is 3:02 PM central time, and this is Joseph Green in San Antonio, Texas, speaking with Mrs. Insured P. Insured about an auto accident. Mrs. Insured, do you understand that we are being recorded? And do I have your permission to do so?"

Again, your introduction will vary, but it will have at least that much information. Some companies like more extensive introductions.

INFORMATION

All statements are going to require some basic information. No matter what the claim, you're going to need to know some basic stuff: the person's name, their relationship to the claim, whether they were driving or a passenger, where they lives, their phone number, and driver's license and date of birth. Medical claims – injuries – require a social security number, and sometimes claims organizations require you to ask everybody for one. But that all makes sense, right? You have to know that stuff.

What's next? The accident scene. What day did it happen? What time? Was it on a road or a parking lot? If on a road, how many lanes are on the road? Which lane was the person on? Were there lights or a stop sign? How fast was the person going?

Once you've figured out the North-South-East-West coordinates and where everybody was located, you can ask the person to describe the accident in their words.

When you ask that question, you will then need to actively listen to what they are saying and react to it with questions that make sense of the accident. Were there any obstructions? Did they see the other car? (People love to say "They came out of nowhere!" I think they think it sounds like the person was going so fast no one could have avoided the accident. In fact, it means they weren't paying attention. Cars don't normally materialize and de-materialize like the Tardis.)

You then need to get information about the passengers, how they know the passengers, and whether there were any injuries and, if so, what those injuries were. Was there a police report? Was anyone transported? Where was the car towed to? (This is a very important question. If the car was towed, the first order of business is to get the car moved out of there, because costs associated with tow yards get way out of hand very quickly). Eventually you get to a point where you wrap things up.

You want to make sure you ask the person if they have anything else to add, or did you cover everything about the accident? Then you do an outro which is basically the reverse of your intro. "This was Joe Green speaking with Mrs. Insured, it is now 3:26 PM and with your permission I will now turn off the recorder," or something similar.

In my play, THE VAPOURS, there is an accident investigator who is up in the Pacific Northwest and she ends up talking to a young woman who doesn't want to give too many details about her accident. Of course, I had to alter the format a little for the purposes of drama but it does give you a pretty good idea of how it's supposed to work. It goes like this:

```
She turns on the recorder.

CRISTABEL
This is Cristabel Cuellar speaking
with Judith MacManus in Acheron,
```

Washington, on May 15, 2009, about an incident that occurred on April 12, 2009. Miss MacManus, do you understand this conversation is being recorded?

JUDITH
Yes.

CRISTABEL
And do I have your permission to do so?

JUDITH
Yes.

CRISTABEL
Great. Please state your full name and spell your last name for me.

JUDITH
Judith MacManus, M-A-C-M-A-N-U-S.

CRISTABEL
And your address?

JUDITH
903 Hellam Place, Acheron,

Washington.
CRISTABEL
What is your date of birth?

JUDITH
June 17, 1987.

CRISTABEL
Thank you. Now, I will focus my
questions on the evening of April 12,
2009. I want to get a sense of what
happened, in as much detail as we can
get.

CRISTABEL
So you said it was dark out –

JUDITH
Yes. I had to use my headlights. That
particular road is so dark at night.

CRISTABEL
Which road?

JUDITH
Old Saint John's.

CRISTABEL
How many lanes are on that road?

JUDITH
Um, one. One for each direction. It's
very narrow.

CRISTABEL
How fast were you going?

JUDITH
About 35, I think?

CRISTABEL
And what would be the speed limit on
that road?

JUDITH
Oh, I think it's a 45? Is it a 45?
There's a sign. I think so.

CRISTABEL
How was traffic?

JUDITH
None at all...

CRISTABEL
Ah...If you would, just tell me in your
own words what happened?

JUDITH
Sure. As I said, I was going about 35
miles per hour, just going along,
like I've done a hundred times up to
Hopelove - up to the church.
Everything seemed fine. It was foggy
of course - the fog gets thick up
here, combination of our climate and
the elevation - we call it the
vapors. Anyway I was driving, and -
I, I, made a hard swerve to the
right, spun into the grass, ended up
scraping against a tree. That's when
it stopped. I was kinda shaken up at
that point, but basically all right.
(Pause) I called Marge Deacon on my
cell and she and her husband came out
to get me.

CRISTABEL
All right. I'm sorry, I'm not quite
understanding - what caused you to
swerve?

JUDITH
Hm?

CRISTABEL
What caused you to swerve?

JUDITH
Well, when I swerved initially, I just got onto the grass and the car wouldn't obey - the tires couldn't get hooked or whatever, I just lost control - because I hit the grass. It was wet out, so the thing just kept sliding. Sliding and sliding.

CRISTABEL
Yeah. But what actually made you swerve?

JUDITH
I must have lost control of the car.

CRISTABEL
So you were driving along, and everything is fine, and then fifteen seconds later you were in a tree.

JUDITH
Yes.

CRISTABEL
Did you hit anything else?

JUDITH

No. I don't think so.

CRISTABEL
Did you hit an animal?

JUDITH
An animal?

CRISTABEL
Yes.

JUDITH
I don't think - I don't remember. I
think I would remember that.

Anyway, you find out that Judith hit something rather peculiar, but for that's another story.

In the back of the book, I have some questions that might make up a typical recorded statement. Every company does more or less the same thing but with little differences, so this is just to give you some idea of how it goes.

The most important thing is to get the details straight. Especially at first, you will always forget to ask some question or another. It's OK. You get to practice this as you go, and you get better.

You'll probably make some screw ups. It happens. You make it and then you fix it and move on.

Keep in mind: any statement is better than no statement.

When I was a baby adjuster, my first year, I took a coworker call for another, more experienced adjuster. I got a statement for her and dropped off the cassette on her desk (again, this was the old days. No, I didn't ride a horse to work.)

Later that afternoon she came by my desk, furious, telling at me. She called my boss over as well. "I want you to hear this." She got down, put the cassette in, and played the tape. The part that made her mad was when I asked the person whether they were injured. It went something like this:

ME
Were you injured at all, ma'am?

INSURED
Yes. I had whiplash and we visited the hospital that night.

ME

Okay, great. What color was the car?

Not good.

I don't know what I was thinking. Probably multi-tasking and definitely failing to actively listen. Or even passively listen. I was just going through my statement form. Whatever, it was a screw up.

Here's the thing, though. Going over to my desk, calling my boss over, and making a production about bitching me out in front of God and everybody? That wasn't cool. In fact, my boss told me not to worry about it. *Just don't do it again.*

Okay.

Another thing, since we're talking.

Calling out your coworkers for making mistakes is just not professional. Especially when you're doing a favor for them. Did I hose that statement? Yup. Was the adjuster going to have to go back and get those details I missed? Yup. Was it the end of the world? No.

I used to play poker with the adjusters that taught

me how to do the job, and every now and then they'd remind me. "Hey Joe, I was trying to remember – what color was the car?" Breaking balls, these guys.

I'm not excusing mistakes. Far from it. But you will make them. Fix them, but don't beat yourself up about it. And especially, after you get some experience, don't go looking to kill somebody else because they erred. (Unless they make a habit of it…) Don't get me wrong. I've worked with incompetent adjusters. I once worked for a boss who wouldn't fire an adjuster if they screwed up 100 times. They could come to work drunk and dressed like Batman and never get canned.

In the claims world, a bad file is often referred to as a **dog**. Means many things. Sometimes it means that the situation is bad – we have a claim with a bunch of excess exposures, or we insure somebody famous who did something stupid – and sometimes it means it was just a regular file that turned into dog through mishandling. Used to know a guy who screwed up so many files his nickname was Kennel Master.

And yet, like with any other office environment,

stuff happens. In general it's better to work well with others. Don't beat someone up just because they torpedoed the statement, and certainly don't document your negative observations about what someone else did on your file. Work it out with the individual. Everyone will be better for it.

Bottom line – almost any statement is better than no statement.

COUPLE OF POINTS

Two points to remember when taking statements: (1) don't talk about insurance, and (2) don't talk to insureds about their DWI if they are charged with it.

The reason you try not to talk about insurance is because if the case ever goes to a court, insurance often cannot be mentioned in proceedings. The idea is that if the jury hears that there is insurance it may affect their civil awards. Obviously, very few cases go to court, so this is a minor concern. However, insurance is typically not relevant the statement so there's no reason to get into all that.

The second point may be more controversial. If my

insured on a particular claim was arrested or had a DWI situation, I would not typically ask about the citation or arrest. Part of the reason is that doing so can end up getting you, as an adjuster, named in a DWI hearing. It's happened to a friend of mine, where he was dragged into court to testify against his insured. And he didn't even ask the insured about it – the guy volunteered it! What can you do?

The other reason goes to the broader part of what we do as adjusters. As an adjuster, you are not the lawyer for the insured. But having said that, I do think as a general rule that one shouldn't knowingly take actions that will potentially harm the insured. There are even situations where it might be advisable to waive a recorded statement for the insured. If you know the statement is going to be "I was smoking my crack pipe with my tiger on the front seat and the tiger really wanted to drive, so I figured, you know, he was sober…" We probably don't need to put that in stone. It will already be in the police report anyway.

Like everything else in claims handling, use your head. And if you're not sure, ask somebody.

SETTLING SIMPLE CLAIMS

When you start handling auto claims, the odds are you will be settling minor claims with no liability or coverage issues. A typical entry-level claims position is very phone intensive, and involves juggling a lot of small claims that are easy to resolve.

The kinds of claims you will see are Comprehensive losses, as well as Collision losses in which only one car is involved. The most common types of Comprehensive losses are wind/hail, deer collision, rain (as in somebody left the top down or a window open), and partial theft.

Partial theft? What the heck is a partial theft?

There are two types of theft claims when you're talking about automobiles. A **total theft** means the whole car got stolen. A **partial theft** means that the car was broken into and something was stolen from the car, like a stereo or loose items.

An introductory claims adjuster will handle partial thefts, but never total thefts. The reason for that is typically total thefts and total fires typically are handled by a special unit, since there is a more prevalent element of crime in both types of claims. The recorded statements for these claims are much longer than a regular recorded statement and are sometimes done in person. When I worked as a private eye, I frequently did in-person interviews for car thefts, especially near the border. That meant driving down to Laredo or Zapata and talking to somebody who may or may not have stolen a car to get out from under an onerous payment or just because they're hoping for some quick cash.

The main thing you need to know about partial thefts is that you have to look at the policy language under the Comprehensive coverage. Depending on the language and the type of policy, it's likely that only a **permanently attached electronic device** will be covered, and only up to a certain limit, like $1200 or so. Loose items – like clothes, your laptop, whatever – are not typically covered under an auto policy. They might be covered under a homeowner's or renter's policy, but that's another story. An auto policy isn't meant to cover stuff that isn't an actual part of the car.

When I worked for a certain insurance company back in the day, and they handled a certain military base, we started getting flooded with partial theft claims. One of their buddies got paid on a stereo claim and suddenly we were inundated with grunts telling us about their broken-into cars. "And I had my laptop in there, and er, my TV, and a set of golf clubs, and, er, a fur coat, and…" And we'd tell them, there's no coverage for that stuff.

"Oh."

Anyway, usually on small claims like this you're taking a statement, getting a police report case number, getting the proof of payment from the insured, and issuing a check less the deductible.

ISSUING PAYMENTS

When you issue a payment, the only things you will need to get are some type of proof of ownership (which theoretically the agent will get, but you'd be surprised how many idiot insurance companies don't *require* proof of ownership) and a clear title if they want the check made out to them alone.

So, proof of ownership. What you want to see is a bill of sale – the piece of paper that says the person who has the insurance policy actually owns the car in question.

Wait. Why would someone want to insure a car they don't own?

There are several reasons, but let's look at a typical scenario. Grandma buys a car for her grandson and buys an insurance policy for the car. Grandma pays the bills, but the car resides with grandson. Everybody wins, right?

No. The insurance company is charging a rate that is based on Grandma driving the car at her house, not grandson driving the car at his house, with his buddies, drag racing his Honda Civic loaded on half a quart of Mad Dog 20/20. This happens all the time.

Anyway, proof of ownership is important.

TITLE

Insurance companies also want to see a title before they issue payment. The reason is most vehicles are obviously not purchased straight cash. A bank, lending agent, or dealership is involved, and they stand to lose out if the car gets totaled wherein they haven't been paid off. They are therefore listed as a **lienholder** on the title.

If there is a lienholder, normally checks need to be issue to the listed owner of the vehicle and the lienholder, or in some cases a body shop. Depends on the individual carrier.

There are many scenarios for this sort of thing to happen. Often for older vehicles, someone buys a car from someone else on Auto Trader and they never bother to change the title.

DEER COLLISION

Out in rural areas, especially in Texas, deer like to run across the road in the wee hours of the morning and get crushed by enormous Dodge trucks. These wrecks can sometimes be serious, but assuming no one is hurt, entry-level claims adjusters will handle these types of losses.

Usually the statement for a deer hit is fairly simple, and you are just trying to confirm the date of loss, the ownership of the car, the policy coverage, and then get the vehicle repaired and paid. And you don't need a statement from the animal, because they're probably demised and you don't speak deer.

A deer collision is not considered an at-fault accident. It's Comprehensive – like any wreck with an animal.

While we are on the subject, however, you should understand that obviously deer don't belong to people. At least not usually – they're not common pets, and we don't use deer for anything in Texas except to shoot at and eat or put their antlers up in the den.

What about cows? What if you hit a cow? Cows

usually belong to someone. Does the owner of a cow owe for your damage, or do you owe the owner for the loss of the cow?

Any ideas?

It depends.

It actually depends on whether the county you are in is considered a "open range" county" or a "closed range" county. See, in 1893 the Texas Supreme Court said *Texas was an open range state, but in the intervening years it also said there could be local exceptions*. Confusing? Yup. So some areas of Texas are handled as closed range. The answer in any particular situation is in the stock laws, and they are not on the Internet. To find out whether an area is open range or closed range, you will need to call the County Commissioner's Office of the county where the accident happened. The answer to that question means a great deal, since either you owe the cow or the cow owes you. And cows can get expensive.

This is only the beginning, as it can get quite complicated depending on the type of animal, or whether local laws allow people to let animals run near their property, and how much effort they have to put into keeping their gates in repair, etc. I've only had a handful of these claims over the years, but they always require doing a bit of research to find out. Good luck when you get one.

You should also check out the film *Open Range*, which is about the battle between the large stockyards, who defended private property, and the freegrazers, who moved cattle across the country. Plus is has a hell of gunfight at the end.

HAIL

Hail claims are usually pretty simple to handle and sometimes are considered a "catastrophe," in which a lot of the same type of claims come in and so they are grouped together. A hailstorm hits a large city like Dallas, so insurance companies put a "catastrophe" tag on it and often engage all their employees to clearing them out.

GETTING THE ESTIMATE

There are several ways to get an estimate for a vehicle when it's damaged. The most common way is through a drive-in location. These will either be managed by a shop that works with the insurance company, or by appraisers working for the insurance company. In either case, the insured (or claimant) gets an estimate and then can take it to the shop of their choice.

Not often done anymore, companies used to have people obtain three estimates and then use the least expensive one. Some people might do that on their own because they've heard that's how it is done, but usually that isn't the case.

The other ways to get an estimate are through a preferred shop or via a field appraisal. A preferred shop is a shop that works with a particular company and will repair the vehicle. A field appraiser is someone who goes out to look at the car where it's located. This is done in remote areas or sometimes if the vehicle is a possible total loss and not drivable.

Once the estimate is obtained and repairs completed, the adjuster issues a check either to the owner, the body shop, the lienholder, or one of more of these to settle the claim.

Property damage releases are not typically taken

unless there is a danger of going over the PD limit of the insured or if there is that possibility.

A property damage release is just a document that a claimant would sign agreeing that the amount paid settles the claim completely and bars further claims.

LIMITS CASES

Supposing your insured has a $25,000 limit of their Property Damage coverage with Redfox Insurance, but they wreck an SUV worth $35,000.00. The vehicle is a total loss.

If the claimant has insurance, it's usually better for the claimant to file with their own carrier, settle the loss, and then their insurance will subrogate against the at-fault party's insurance. Subrogate means to seek reimbursement from. So in the above example, the claimant files with her own carrier – Cavalier Insurance – and settles out the claim, pays her deductible, and then Cavalier subrogates. They make a **subrogation demand** (more on those later) against Redfox Insurance for $35,000. Redfox says, we only have $25,000. Cavalier has to make a decision to either take the $25K or try to go after the insured's personal assets. 99% of the time, the carrier will take the $25K, sign a release, and eat the $10 K.

Limits cases can get very complicated if there are more than two parties. However, especially at first, you won't handle losses like that.

WHAT WE OWE

While we're on the subject, however, remember that the Property Damage coverage covers everything to which the insured becomes liable. That doesn't just mean a vehicle. What if your insured hits a house? If there's a hole in the living room, the people might not be able to live there. So they need to stay in a hotel. That would be covered under the PD.

What if the insured hits a vehicle that a farmer uses to sell tomatoes out of? He doesn't have a business while his truck is in the shop. You'd owe him a rental, sure, but maybe you owe him for some lost business as well.

Don't get stuck in only thinking about cars and trucks and such. That's most of your job, but every claim is different.

Also, we have to take into consideration the person's circumstances. One time my insured hit a paraplegic with a special van set up with hand controls to drive the vehicle. We had to get the claimant one for rental, at some expense.

We don't always owe for exactitude – we don't necessarily owe someone a fancy sedan just because they drive one – usually a vehicle of the same size. But every claim is different and some will make you think out of the box. And that's OK.

As an adjuster, you are tasked with handling all claims in the spirit of **good faith and fair dealing**. What that means may vary according to the situation, but in general it means make your best effort to treat everybody fairly. Treat people like you would want to be treated. Be straight with people and give them all their options without directing them to one or the other.

I used to tell my students, **the odds are your particular case will never end up in court, but it's not a bad idea to behave as if they will be.** Is that thing you said something you wouldn't mind being read to a jury? Would you be comfortable with that paragraph you just documented in the file being read to a jury? If not, then maybe you should rethink what you're saying or documenting. Not a bad thing to keep in mind when you're adjusting.

LIABILITY

A big part of your job will involve determining who is liable for a given accident. Many times it will be relatively simple. Other times it will be almost impossible to determine. When we say someone is liable, we are saying who is responsible for the accident. Whose behavior led to the collision occurring?

How do we determine liability? We use evidence. So what constitutes evidence?

Let's imagine that we have a two-vehicle accident. In the accident we are looking at, Vehicle A is trying to get out of a parking lot and is sitting at the exit. Vehicle A starts to move forward, then has to stop due to a pedestrian crossing in front of the car. Vehicle B, which was behind Vehicle A, starts up and is unable to stop before crashing into the rear Vehicle A.

The liability refers to potential damages you would owe to a third party. If you remember, **a third party is anyone who is not a party to your insurance contract.**

Liability is divided into two sections: BODILY INJURY and PROPERTY DAMAGE.

Bodily Injury refers to any sort of physical harm done to another person.

POLICE REPORTS

Wait, don't all accidents have police reports? And don't the police officers determine who is at fault?

Not necessarily. First of all, many accidents will not have a police report. In some metropolitan areas, good luck getting the cops to come out unless there's a body. Minor fender benders, they might or might not. Depends on how busy they are, or how far away they have a patrol unit. Also note

that if an accident happens on private property –
like a department store parking lot, for example –
officers won't normally come out but even if they
do, they won't usually write a report. And there's a
good reason for this – care to guess?

No?

*Because traffic laws are designed for public roads
and don't apply to parking lots.*

What about stop signs inside mall parking lots?
And aren't there speed limits?

Technically, they don't mean a thing. Now as a
practical matter you can still be criminally
negligent, so don't go 75 at WAL-MART.

So no, there will often not be a police report for the
accidents you handle.

But let's say you do have a police report. A typical
police report will have a section that tells you who
the drivers were, a narrative of how the officer
thinks the accident happened based on his
investigation, and some factors. The factors
determine who he thinks was at fault. On a San

Antonio Police Department report, some common factors are:

20 – DRIVER INATTENTION

This is one you'll see all the time. Most accidents are caused by one or more persons not paying attention to the road. So you'll see this factor all the time.

4 – CHANGED LANES WHEN UNSAFE

Another common one. One car is in its lane, properly moving, and another car changes lanes into it. The driver of the vehicle changing lanes has a responsibility to make sure the way is clear before coming over. That makes intuitive sense, doesn't it?

60 – UNSAFE SPEED

Note the words. "Unsafe" speed. Just because someone drives under the speed limit doesn't make it safe to do so. If the roads were iced over, and the speed limit was 30, and you are going 20, but you lose control of the car and careen into someone's yard, guess what? 20 was an unsafe speed, because you were not able to keep control of the vehicle.

Those are just a few examples. There are police overlays available for study on the Internet. Follow the website shown at the end of this book to find links to this and many other useful items.

INVESTIGATION

A word about investigating a claim, because this is something I always told my students to do. If you want to know how to investigate something, watch the old TV program *Columbo*. Columbo was played by the great Peter Falk, who gave great performances in many John Cassavetes films and played the grandpa in *The Princess Bride*, but became primarily identified with the one character of Columbo.

And no wonder. No less than Stephen Fry has said that Columbo is one of the great characters of Western drama, comparable to Shakespeare's Falstaff. And if you follow his techniques you will go far in this job.

The most important aspect of Columbo that I like my students to borrow is how he handles confrontation. Whenever Columbo is asking questions about a case, he is perpetually confused. He takes one fact that someone says, and takes another fact that someone says, expresses bewilderment because they don't match, and politely asks the person in question to please clarify if possible. That is a wonderful tactic. There is no need to immediately go to confrontation is most situations, and it is much better to give everyone the benefit of the doubt and allow them to explain their way out of apparent contradictions. Or not.

I'm serious. Watch an episode or two.

Okay, back to business.

At minimum, if we understand five key aspects of any particular accident, we will be on our way to making a good, solid liability decision. That is not to say that we will always have this information, or that this information is the only thing necessary for all claims. The nature of claims is that every situation is unique. Our objective is to use all available information to the best of our ability to achieve a fair, defensible conclusion.

1) RIGHT OF WAY:

The main question to ask is: Is right of way favorable for the insured or the claimant? Is it not applicable? (For example, in a parking lot accident right of way may not be an issue). Or is it unknown? (Not enough information to say.)

Typically, a person who is already established in a lane of travel has right of way over a person who is trying to change their lane. A person headed straight will typically have right of way over a person turning left in front of them (unless they have a protected green arrow or similar situation). A person already on a given road will have a right of way over a person exiting a business to get on that road, and so on.

Many times a person who turns left in front of another vehicle (without right of way) will allege speed on the part of the other vehicle. That is fine, but remember a couple of things: (1) Speed is very hard to prove, and (2) Speed isn't going to affect the liability much, unless the speed is so outrageous that it becomes obviously so negligent as to be the primary cause of the crash. Which means are likely seriously injured. Speed will not normally be a factor you can prove in a minor accident and will play little to no role in your liability determination.

2) CONTROL OF ROAD:

Who has control of the road? Do we have possession of the intersection or road at the time of the accident?

Having control of the road is similar to right of way, but it applies even in situations where right of way is not clear. For example, take a four-way-stop situation where the insured and claimant are disputing who ran the stop sign. Without any witnesses or a police report, we may not be able to draw a conclusion about right of way. However, imagine that our insured vehicle has damage to the left quarter panel and the claimant's damages are to the front end. We might feel, based upon this evidence, that our insured was out into the intersection first and therefore had control of the road. Although it doesn't prove that we didn't run the stop sign, it does prove that we had gotten further out than the claimant at the time of the accident, which could cause us to wonder why they didn't see the insured vehicle. Control of road, in this instance, would be favorable to the insured.

3) EVASIVE ACTION:

Did either party do anything to avoid the accident? Note: honking your horn (as in a parking lot accident) can be considered "evasive action."

Evasive actions are ones taken to avoid, or reduce the consequences of, an accident. This can get tricky in liability cases. For example, let's say the claimant turned left in front of the insured, and the insured struck the claimant at the very edge of the claimant's quarter panel. One could argue that the claimant had claimed possession of the lane and the insured could have avoided the accident altogether, seeing as how it only barely scraped the claimant vehicle. However, suppose we get statements and it turned out the insured barely hit the claimant because the insured driver made a hard swerve to avoid and almost did so. In other words, it was not the insured's carelessness but the insured's logical action that minimized the damage to the claimant vehicle.

4) AWARENESS:

When did each party first become aware of the other? Did they react (for example, by slowing down) upon seeing the other vehicle? Remember that in certain situations, the importance of driver awareness becomes intensified – when backing, for example, or driving in a residential neighborhood.

Awareness is an important aspect of any accident. Typically, at least one person is not paying enough attention if a pair of vehicles end up colliding with one another.

5) POINT OF IMPACT:

Is the point of impact favorable? If we have an intersection accident where both the insured and claimant are stating the other party ran a stop sign, for example, if the claimant struck our insured T-bone style in the side of the vehicle, that is a favorable situation for the insured. The insured, in this case, got further out into the intersection than the claimant did. If the claimant states we rear-ended them but both vehicles have damage to the side, the points of impact do not match the story and the situation may become favorable to us.

LIABILITY DEFINITION

Liability means to be legally obligated or

responsible. For the purpose of claims handling, insurance representatives determine who is legally liable or, put simply, who is at fault. Liability insurance policies require insurers to accept the financial consequences of their insured's liability.

Liability accidents are typically investigated by using recorded statements from relevant individuals, a police report if there is one, the estimate and photos of the vehicles involved, scene photos, and more depending on the loss details. Some accidents may be very simple and others complex, and some accidents that seem simple at first turn into big complicated things.

NEGLIGENCE

Negligence can typically be thought of as carelessness. This is often expressed as "X failed to exercise due care." We owe a general degree of care to other people for our own actions.

So, for example, in terms of negligence:

If you show that you were careful and the other person was careless (negligent), that person is liable for any reasonable, relevant damage.

If an accident is caused by dangerous property or by a defective product, the owner of the property or the maker or seller of the product is liable regardless of whether he or she actually created the danger or defect. This can come into play on our files where we have a tire defect, or the particular failure or a seatbelt system or brake system. Although this should be rare, we need to be aware that sometimes product liability can become an issue.

An individual who was also careless, but to a lesser degree than another party, can have their right to be compensated reduced or eliminated in some cases. This is referred to as **"comparative negligence."** In other words, one's carelessness (negligence) is weighed against the carelessness of another person.

These are some of the more common types of negligence as they relate to auto accidents:

DRIVER INATTENTION

The most basic thing that someone can do wrong in a vehicle, a driver who is inattentive can be guilty of negligence because he or she was distracted. A driver who is attending to a small child in the vehicle, changing radio stations, cleaning up spilled coffee, or any of a thousand different things can become inattentive as a result. Using your cell phone is a special kind of inattention – this is sometimes illegal by itself, as in California.

IMPROPER LOOKOUT

Lookout refers to the ability for a certain driver to see what is happening. For example, any driver that is in a vehicle behind another vehicle should have better lookout than the vehicle in front. That's one of the reasons rear-ending a vehicle is often considered the fault of the driver of the car behind.

FAILURE TO YIELD (FTYROW)

This is also a basic type of negligence, where a driver fails to yield right-of-way to another driver. This falls under many different categories:
- FTYROW – turning left
- FTYROW – stop sign
- FTYROW – traffic light
- FTYROW – from private drive

These are just examples. There could be other

variations.

FAILURE TO CONTROL SPEED (FTCS) DRIVING TOO FAST FOR CONDITIONS FAILURE TO MAINTAIN ASSURED CLEAR DISTANCE

Failure to Control Speed is not the same as "speeding." Speeding is very difficult to prove. However, the key issue is often whether the person was driving too fast for conditions, even if it is within the technical speed limit. For example, let's suppose there is a huge snowstorm with icy conditions at the time of the accident. The speed limit is 30, and the claimant was going 25. Based on conditions, 25 might have been too fast, even though that speed was technically legal. As we might recall, legality is not the same thing as negligence.

IMPROPER LANE CHANGE (or CHANGED LANES WHEN UNSAFE)

The person who changes lanes into a vehicle that is already established in a given lane will be negligent. This will usually be noted as an Improper Lane Change, because the vehicle movement was made while it was not safe to do so.

IMPROPER TURN

Not all turns are Failure to Yield type turns. If, in the course of turning, the insured were to strike a parked car for example, we would call that an Improper Turn. Once again, this was a movement made by a vehicle that was not done safely.

BACKED UNSAFELY

Backing a vehicle is an inherently dangerous maneuver. Whenever a person is backing out, their lookout is compromised because they have to rely on mirrors as well as craning their head around. Also, backing is often done in places frequented by pedestrians – parking lots, neighborhoods, and highly crowded and tight areas. Backing therefore means that a driver has a high degree of care owed.

FAULTY EVASIVE ACTION

This is when a driver overreacts to something on the road or otherwise has a bad reaction to an incident on the road. For example, a driver who feels that the vehicle to his right is moving toward him so they pull onto oncoming traffic has made a very poor decision. It might also refer to a driver who fails to hit his or her horn before being struck by a backing vehicle, given sufficient time to do so. (Honking a horn is considered evasive action – it's an action whose purpose is to avoid an accident.)

FAILURE TO MAINTAIN CONTROL OF THE VEHICLE

Suppose a driver thinks that a car is coming out of a private drive, but reacts by changing lanes and then losing control of the car, so that it careens wildly into a tree. The driver failed to maintain control of the vehicle, which is as basic a duty as there is while driving.

All these negligence types can be combined. For example, someone running a stop sign might be guilty of both FTYROW and Improper Lookout (if they didn't see the sign). It's perfectly OK to find more than one negligent action on an insured or claimant driver.

This list is also not meant to be exhaustive. These are just some of the major issues that you will run into over and over again when making liability decisions.

EXCESS SITUATIONS

Another thing you have to be on the lookout for is a potential excess situation. What does that mean? Well, say for example your insured hits a BMW and then pushes it into a brand new SUV, and none of the vehicles are drivable. Imagine the insured has a $25,000 maximum limit for Property Damage.

Remember, that's all you've got. If the damages from the accident go over that $25,000, the insured has a potential exposure to his or her own assets. That means they could get sued, which means your job is going to be to try and settle all available claims while also protecting your insured as best you can.

First thing is to identify those claims. In this example, we want to warn the insured about the potential exposure as soon as we are aware. We would normally send an *excess letter* – putting this warning in writing for our insured.

TYPES OF NEGLIGENCE

Different states have different methods of assessing liability. When I say assessing liability, I mean looking at types of accidents and making decisions about who is responsible.

For example, let's take a simple accident in which Vehicle A is sitting at a red stop light and Vehicle B strikes it from behind. Vehicle A did nothing wrong and Vehicle B failed to maintain a proper speed, or failed to maintain lookout. However you want to say it, Vehicle B did not stop when it needed to before striking Vehicle A. So your liability assessment might look like the following:

Vehicle A: 0%
Vehicle B: 100% - failed to control speed

Vehicle B owes 100% of Vehicle A's damages.

Make sense?

Let's take a slightly different accident. Let's imagine Vehicle A was traveling at a high rate of speed when Vehicle B decided to turn left in front of Vehicle B at an open intersection.

With no traffic lights or signals, vehicles turning left are expected to yield right-of-way to vehicles coming in the other direction going straight. However, after investigating the accident you determine that Vehicle A was traveling 15 MPH over the listed limit. You feel that Vehicle A has contributed to the accident, even though Vehicle B is primarily at fault. (Incidentally, speed is very difficult to prove unless the person admits they were speeding or they receive a citation for it. It is possible to get speed from an engineer's report, but doing a full report will be very rare and only in serious cases, because they're expensive.)

So in this case: (let's say)

Vehicle A: 20% at fault – speeding over limit
Vehicle B: 80% at fault – FTYROW turning left

One party is 20% at fault and the other is 80% at fault? How does that work?

The answer is "it depends." It depends on what state you're in.

Let's begin with Texas. The Texas way to assess liability is called MODIFIED COMPARATIVE

FAULT, or sometimes NOT GREATER THAN. In the Texas system, in order to collect, your degree of fault must not be "greater than" the other person.

Here's an easy way to think about it. Imagine that you back out of a parking space right at the same time the person across from you is backing out, and you both back into each other without seeing the other. You decide, in this situation, that both parties share liability equally – they both owe 50% of the loss. In Texas, that means both parties literally owe 50% of the other's damages.

This is also sometimes referred to as 51% Bar, as in *51% of fault means you are barred from recovery.*

Note that doesn't mean the owe equal *money*. They owe equal *damages*. If a Porsche and a Hyundai back into each other, the amount of damage will likely not be the same. **But each party owes 50% of the other's damages**. The difference could be thousands of dollars.

So, in our original example, we had Vehicle A at 20% at fault and Vehicle B at 80% at fault. Vehicle B therefore owes 80% of the damages to Vehicle A. Vehicle A owes 0% of the damages to Vehicle

B. Why? **Because Vehicle B's degree of fault is greater than Vehicle A.**

As a practical matter, that means if you are at least 51% at fault in an accident in Texas, **you cannot collect**.

Most states have that form of MODIFIED COMPARATIVE FAULT. There is another form of MODIFIED COMPARATIVE FAULT. It is exactly like Texas, except that it says that your degree of fault must be "less than" the other person.

The only practical difference is in the 50-50 type accident we just looked at. In an accident where you determine that people share fault equally (Vehicle A and Vehicle B are both 50% responsible), **nobody gets paid**.

This is also sometimes referred to as 50% Bar, as in *50% of fault means you are barred from recovery.*

Remember this only applies to Property Damage. Collision coverage is no-fault so you can always make a Collision claim on your own policy and pay the deductible.

There are two other types of comparative fault in use in the United States. (Well, technically three – South Dakota uses something called Slight-Gross, but if you ever end up South Dakota claims for some reason you'll need to use local sources to help with it.)

The other types of comparative fault are PURE and CONTRIBUTORY NEGLIGENCE. Many states are PURE; there are only five CONTRIBUTORY NEGLIGENCE states, and most of them are on the East coast.

PURE

Pure means that everyone owes their exact degree of fault, no matter how small, as long as it is above zero. California is Pure.

So if you have an accident where you determine that one person is 1% at fault, and the other is 99% at fault, then they each pay each other according their degree of fault. The person who is 99% at fault can collect 1% from the other person. (As a practical matter, this doesn't really happen much for two vehicle claims, obviously.)

You are never barred from recovery in this model unless you are 100% at fault. So this is 100% Bar.

CONTRIBUTORY NEGLIGENCE

Contributory states are quite simple. If you are at fault, AT ALL, by 1% or more, you CANNOT collect. One person is 99% at fault, the other is 1% at fault, nobody gets paid. Sound unfair? It's a little extreme, but it is easy to work with as an adjuster. An example of such a state is North Carolina.

This is also sometimes referred to as 1% Bar, as in *1% of fault means you are barred from recovery.*

As a rule of thumb, the states that follow CONTRIBUTORY NEGLIGENCE are mostly in the East, while most of the middle of the country have either form of the MODIFIED COMPARATIVE, while as you move west across the country PURE becomes popular. And this makes sense historically, since are oldest laws come from the east coast since the colonists expanded westward. As they expanded, they used new approaches to laws rather than the somewhat simple CONTRIBUTORY NEGLIGENCE standard.

So going all the way back to our 80-20 accident, where Vehicle A was 20% at fault and Vehicle B was 80% at fault, we can see who collects based on the four types of negligence.

MODIFIED COMPARATIVE (NOT GREATER THAN)

Vehicle A: collects 80% of his damages, owes 0%
Vehicle B: collects zero, pays 80% of A's damages

MODIFIED COMPARATIVE (LESS THAN)

Vehicle A: collects 80% of his damages, owes 0%
Vehicle B: collects zero, pays 80% of A's damages

PURE

Vehicle A: collects 80%, owes 20% of B's damages
Vehicle B: collects 20%, pays 80% of A's damages

CONTRIBUTORY NEGLIGENCE

Vehicle A: collects zero, owes 0%
Vehicle B: collects zero, owes 0% of A's damages

Complete list of states and the Negligence they use:

PURE (% of fault)

Alaska
Arizona
California
Florida
Kentucky
Louisiana
Missouri
Mississippi
New Mexico
New York
Rhode Island
Washington

CONTRIBUTORY NEGLIGENCE (1% Bar)

Alabama
District of Columbia
Maryland
North Carolina
Virginia

MODIFIED COMPARATIVE FAULT (50% Bar)

Arkansas
Colorado
Georgia
Idaho
Kansas
Maine
Nebraska
North Dakota
Tennessee
Utah

MODIFIED COMPARATIVE FAULT (51% Bar)

Connecticut
Delaware
Hawaii
Illinois
Indiana
Iowa
Massachusetts
Michigan
Minnesota
Montana
Nevada
New Hampshire
New Jersey
Ohio
Oklahoma

Oregon
Pennsylvania
South Carolina
Texas
Vermont
West Virginia
Wisconsin
Wyoming

WALKING THROUGH A CLAIM

Let's break down what you need to do when you first receive a claim all the way through. We will start with a simple claim. Let's say that you get to work in the morning and the first thing on your desk is a customer who collided with a deer on a country road in Hollywood Park, Texas.

The first question you need to ask is: **Is this a covered loss?** So you will find the date of accident and compare it to the length of the term of the policy. Does the date fall within the term? Let's say the accident happened on October 14, 2017, and the term limits of the policy are September 1, 2017 to February 1, 2017. So that first question is answered Yes.

Next question: **Is this a covered vehicle?** So we look at the vehicle involved in the loss and we look at the vehicles listed on the policy. In this case, it's a 2015 Ford F-150 with the same VIN. (Be very careful with this. People often own more than one of the same vehicle, so you have to make sure you have the right one.)

Next question: **Is this a listed driver?** So we look and we see, indeed, the driver is said to be the Named Insured, Sammy Brown.

So far all the answers are Yes, and we are looking good. But we haven't confirmed anything yet. We are just doing our preliminary assessment. This isn't anything like an actual coverage investigation yet.

Our next step is going to be **get a recorded statement from the driver**, and we want to also **explain coverages to the insured**, and **locate the vehicle**.

That last aspect is extremely important. You need to find the car. If the vehicle is drivable, most of the time the car will be with the insured. That's fine. If the vehicle isn't drivable, we need to know where it's located because we want to move it.

The reason we want to move it is because of storage charges. If a vehicle gets towed to a tow yard or a body shop, they will charge storage fees to keep the vehicle. In some locations (you will find out where), the tow yards are essentially bandits, charging exorbitant fees while holding cars hostage.

Only the owner of a car can move the car. This is very important. We can request the owner move the vehicle, and if the owner doesn't want to cooperate after a certain amount of time we can stop paying fees. (We have to warn the owner first and we can't do this unreasonably – there has to be sufficient time allowed for them to move it.) But insureds and claimants will often be under the impression that we need to move the car **when in fact we cannot move the car**. We don't own the property. They have to give permission for this to happen. In some cases, like if the vehicle is in a police impound lot, they may have to go down there and show a title and/or Driver's License to get the car moved. It's inconvenient but it's how it is.

Depending on whether or not the person has Rental coverage on their policy, and can determine where the vehicle is, you may be able to set up a rental right away. If, however, the vehicle is drivable, the insured will need to get an appointment to drop the vehicle off and only then be able to get a rental. In addition, generally speaking it is better to drop off vehicles early in the week for repair. A vehicle dropped off at a shop on a Friday will not get worked on immediately, as they are trying to finish work that was started earlier in the week or before.

BASIC COVERAGE QUESTIONS

For an auto claim, we need to know that (1) the insurance policy is active, (2) the vehicle is listed on the policy, and (3) the loss is within the scope of the policy. We will also need to determine if there are any potential coverage issues, but these are the basic issues up front. Once we've determined that the loss is confirmed with the date, and the driver ascertained, and a statement obtained, all that remains is set up the insured with an estimate. Once that is obtained and we know how many days the repair will take (based on the estimate), we can then arrange for the payment of the claim and, ultimately, the closure.

Most claims are not that simple, however, and every claim is different. Also, much will depend on the specific company you decide work for. However, this does establish a background of the shape of a claim – what it should more or less look like.

REPAIRING THE VEHICLE

Sometimes repairing the vehicle leads to a dispute when a customer insists on having all brand-new parts or specifically BMW parts for a BMW and so on. Sometimes this is warranted, and almost all insurance companies will use brand new parts for a vehicle less than a year old or up to 12,000-15,000 miles. However, it's not always warranted. I had a guy demand brand new parts for his 2004 BMW with 185,000 miles on it. That's a little unreasonable. Having said that, if a customer insists, and he or she is willing to pay the difference, generally speaking we can do that.

Although usually it's better to get a salvage or refurbished part for an older vehicle. I had a 2001 GMC Sonoma that I drove for 200,000 over 14 years. I had a minor wreck in 2011 which required a door replacement. Would it have made sense to get a 2011 door for my 2001 truck? Not really. There's been ten years of minor changes, and a 2001 door would probably fit better than a 2011. So I got one from a Pick-and-Pull for replacement. It's not just about cost; it's also about fit.

Which leads to the other thing that customers don't like (and body shops don't like sometimes as well): aftermarket parts. **Aftermarket** parts often have a bad reputation in the industry, although I'm not really sure for the reason. An aftermarket part is a part for a vehicle not manufactured by the **Original Equipment Manufacturer** (OEM). It goes something like this:

Ford Motor Company makes tailgates for its line of 2016 Ford Rangers. A company comes along and says, *We want to buy the specs for that tailgate.* Ford sells them the specs, and then they manufacture their own version of the Ford Ranger tailgate, but selling them for a little less. That's an aftermarket part.

You probably have aftermarket parts on your own vehicle, although you may not have thought about it that way. For example, if you replaced the OEM stereo (the stereo the car came with when it was purchased) with say, an Alpine stereo, that is an aftermarket part. When you replaced the tires on your car, did you try to use the tires the car was sold with or did you use whatever they had at Discount Tire? Those are aftermarket parts.

It's like anything else in life. Some aftermarket parts are better than others. However, in general, they just provide more options for car repair, and that's a good thing.

And in my experience, most insurance companies really aren't trying to shaft anybody in the area of car repair. The people in the PD departments tend to be very conscientious and the last thing they want to do is repair a vehicle unsafely or poorly. It's unethical, and it's bad business.

CUSTOMER SERVICE & ETHICS

Customer service in claims is different from other types of work. That's because, in claims, the customer isn't always right. In fact, many times they're wrong, and it's your job to explain *just how and in what ways they are wrong.*

If you think this makes them really happy, you would be incorrect in that judgment.

Having said that, you do have to make the customer happy in whatever way we can do so. That often means explaining the limitations of our powers. We can only do so much. We can't make them not at fault in an accident if they are.

And, now that I mention it, **We** is a very important word.

As in, **We** are together – the insured and I. Especially when the insured is at fault and doesn't think he is. I'll use a lot of We statements. Let's look at some examples.

STUFF INSUREDS LIKE TO SAY

"That guy came out of nowhere. He musta been flying."

People never get tired of saying this. I think they mean it as an excuse, like the other person was going so fast they should be excused from blowing a stop sign, but it's not a point in their favor. It's a sign they weren't paying attention. If you have an accident with someone, and you have absolutely no idea where they came from, and it wasn't from behind, then clearly you weren't aware of your surroundings. Anyway, it's not an excuse.

Now, I wouldn't tell the insured right then that they weren't paying attention. But when it gets down to brass tacks, and we had a stop sign and clobbered a passing vehicle without one, and there's no reason to think speed was a factor on the other party, I will tell the insured: "Let me explain what we have here. Unfortunately, in an accident like this, we had the greater duty since we had a stop sign and the other person didn't. Trouble is, speed is very hard for us to prove. The damage doesn't really support it, and the officer gave us a citation for failing to yield right of way. So if we take this to court, what would a judge say? The judge is going to look at the report and the damage and wonder what we're doing there. It's an unfortunate thing, but in this situation we are going to have pay the other person's damages."

I don't see this as facetious, either. I really do mean **We**. I always see it as my job to protect my insured's interests, and by paying a claim in which he is at fault, that's exactly what I'm doing. I don't mind going to the mattresses for my insured, but we have to have something to build on – some kind of case to present. In the scenario just outlined, we've got nothing. And our job is to break the news gently to our insured.

Speaking of which, setting expectations is very important. If you know we're going to be on the hook, and the insured doesn't think so, go ahead and start laying the groundwork right away. Don't say, "Oh yeah, I'm sure that lady was speeding for sure," in response to his statements. Be objective at first and make a note, but in your head kind in mind we have to prove it. If we can't prove it, then it won't work.

"The kid I rear-ended must have been twelve years old. He couldn't possibly have a license. I know I rear-ended him, but he shouldn't have been on the road!"

or

"That guy was from Mexico. He shouldn't have been driving in the first place, he's an illegal! I know I rear-ended him, but…"

or

"I am 100% sure that guy was drunk off his ass. The cops didn't even do anything, they just let him go. But I could tell just by looking at him he was drunk. I know I rear-ended him, but…"

or

"I think the driver and the passenger switched seats. That seemed really suspicious. When the cops got there, I told them I thought the younger girl was driving, not the other lady. I know I rear-ended them, but…"

You get the idea.

And here's the thing. Only *actions* count when determining fault.

If someone does not have a driver's license, or is not a citizen, or is drunk even, it has nothing to do with the facts of an accident.

Had a claim where a guy was passed out in his car, stopped at a red light at 2AM. Dead drunk. Got rear-ended. Who was at fault? The guy what rear-ended the drunk.

Look at the facts. Did being drunk or asleep contribute to the accident? No. He was stopped at a red light like any other car.

A good way to think about this is that **someone else's status does not award you additional rights.**

If someone is a 15 year old driver playing hooky, and you plow into his vehicle while he is obeying normal traffic laws, you are still at fault.

It's like if you punched somebody on the street, and when the cops came to talk to you, you said, "His car has a handicap sticker." That's irrelevant. Doesn't have to do with anything. I hope we can all agree that we don't get to punch people because they're handicapped.

I've told insureds, we are not the INS. We are not the police. We are not the FBI. By all means they should complain to the proper authorities if they feel strongly about something. And we will always do our normal thorough investigation into any accident. But our proper sphere is insurance. We will work as an insurance company, not an arm of the federal government.

Incidentally, while we are on the subject, whenever you talk to insureds or claimants or anyone, you will be documenting that into the file. "Spoke with insured, explained COLL 500 deductible," etc.

What you won't do is document verbatim what

people tell you. We had a field appraiser once who started doing that in his files. "Customer informed me to insert my head into my a***ole," or "Customer advised that I should go f**k myself."

Don't do that.

"Customer had concerns," will do just fine.

"I know I have \$20 a day in rental coverage, but I can't get an SUV for that."

Unfortunately, we can't authorize over their limit. Best we can do is suggest they talk to the rental agency. We can also, if possible, raise their limit, but that would be for *future* claims, not the present one. Sometimes they're sneaky like that.

When it comes to customer service, I have a very simple mantra: **Be calm, polite, and professional. Give the facts as you know them. If you don't know the answer to a question, put the customer on hold or offer to get the answer and call back. For God's sake, never make anything up.**

Nobody in this business stops asking questions. I've handled all kinds of crazy cases over the years, but I don't know everything. It's impossible. I ask for help when I need it, which is often. That's OK.

Especially at first, when you start taking customer calls you are going to feel like you don't know what you're doing. Everybody feels like that at first. And you're going to make mistakes. The first total loss I ever had, I screwed the pooch nine ways to Sunday. And my very patient insured never even yelled at me about it and we got it fixed. And I did a lot better on my next one.

Don't panic. Don't get angry. The customer isn't always right, remember. You have to say NO a lot in this job. You are always setting the borders for the customer. You *can* do this, you *can't* do that. We *can* do this, we *can't* do that. Over time you will develop a method for handling those explanations, but the most important factor is you need to develop some degree of empathy for the people you talk to. There are going to be tough days in claims, where everybody is screaming at you and everybody wants everything done now. And your job throughout all that is to be calm, polite, and professional. Not to necessarily say yes to every demand the customer makes.

Focus on each phone call as they happen. What do I need to do to end this phone call? Focus on each file as they build. What do I need to do to close this file? The better you get at identifying those things, the more efficient you will be at handling your desk. And efficiency is king in claims.

When you make an appointment with someone on the phone ("I will call you back tomorrow at 2PM") then do it. Following up on your promises will keep you from getting angry calls and voicemails. Customer service is about delivering on promises. Don't set unrealistic expectations – if it's going to take more than a day to get the call back, then say that and explain why. Keep the customer informed.

MINIMUM STANDARDS

Speaking of keeping promises: every state has general claims-handling guidelines that specify how long an insurer has to acknowledge a claim, to respond to a demand from a customer, or how long an insurer has to investigate a claim before settling it. In Texas, these guidelines are set in the Texas Insurance Code. You'll find them at the back of the book.

Failing to meet those mandatory standards can create a situation of **bad faith**. Operating in bad faith with an insured means that treating them in a deceptive or unfair manner. In Texas, bad faith is covered by the Texas Unfair Claims Practices Act. The idea is that when presented with a claim, the insurance adjuster is supposed to settle that claim in a prompt, fair, and equitable manner, and under reasonable circumstances and conditions.

You owe a duty of good faith to your insured by contract and because of the Texas Unfair Claims Practices Act. You don't technically owe precisely the same duty to a third party – at least under Texas law – but as a practical matter you want to treat *everyone* with due respect. (Also, there are some states, like Louisiana, where you can be sued for bad faith by a third party, even though by definition there is no contractual obligation.)

As an adjuster, you are allowed to make mistakes – that is, if you screw up, as long as you fix the mistake, the state will generally acknowledge that these things happen. Making a mistake is not necessarily bad faith. However, making a mistake and then not fixing it, or taking too long to respond to inquiries, or trying to steal or cheat the insured, *does* put you in a position of bad faith. This can lead to lawsuits, and losing your adjusting license, and all sorts of bad things. As Grandmaster Flash and Melle Mel once said about smoking rocks, "Don't do it!"

We don't want to get into trouble. Take care of your customers, treat them respectfully and honestly, and respond in a timely fashion, and you will be just fine.

WHEN YOU'RE GOOD, YOU WILL GET MORE WORK

Here's the bad news about claims.

Like anything else in life, claims adjusters can be outstanding, good, adequate, or just giant balls of suck. Now the better you are at your job, the more work you will get. That is to say, the reward for getting work done is more work. Quite often, you will end up doing the work of people that suck. If management is not in control of flow, you could wind up doing the work of several people that suck.

I once worked at a place where I was in a five-person unit with one good adjuster and three that you could have replaced with ferrets on roller skates and had better productivity. And it got awfully tiring to be told by my boss, "Hey Joe, listen. Do you mind calling this lady back? She's a little upset." Because Ferret #2 was supposed to hike the ball to the quarterback and instead decided to shove the ball up the running back's ass and run to the showers. "Sure," I'd say.

You know why?

Because that's a good situation to be in. Your boss needs messes cleaned up, and she turns to you, that's a pretty good sign of how highly they think of you. Does it get tiring sometimes? Of course. But try to keep in mind: Hopefully, your boss will take care of you down the road. If they can't, then maybe they aren't valuing you properly and you need to take a look at what else is out there.

I would suggest, though, that you eliminate any idea of fairness **in terms of equal treatment for yourself.** You have to be fair at all times to your insureds and claimants, and always behave in a proper manner with them. As I said before, ethics in insurance really revolves around good faith and fair dealing. But that applies to what you do for them. It doesn't have anything to do about your perceptions of fairness to yourself.

Fairness in workload has always been a bear to solve in claims, and it likely never will be solved. Claims is too fast and chaotic to really be fair. Sometimes everybody is slammed, and sometimes it's a little slow. Sometimes you're the one who gets the claim where we blew up a bus with 27 passengers, and sometimes you get nothing but cake claims involving deer hits and such. Luck of the draw. Don't worry about workload too much.

Also, if you're any good, you will be doing more and more complicated work than other people. You want to be the one the Manager says, "Jesus, we nailed a city bus. Why don't we give this one to Joe." Because she knows that you know the football belongs in the quarterback's hands rather than the running back's ass. This is what you want. Because you want to be striving to do more than the minimum. You want to progress. You want to learn more about how to do your job better. You want to kick butt and be the person your boss can rely on. It's not a bad thing at all.

YOUR ADJUSTER LICENSE

When you're first starting off as an adjuster, you need to obtain a license. Specifically, you need a Property and Casualty license from the state of Texas (or the state you are planning to work in). Often insurance companies will train you and get you your license, which is a nice thing, assuming you pass the local test. And once you receive your license, it is good for a certain amount of time (in Texas, two years) before you need to renew your license.

In those two years, you need to complete (in Texas, 24 credit hours worth) of Continuing Education. 2 of those hours must be in Ethics. Again, you must complete them in the time period between obtaining the license and the renewal date. If you don't do that, heavy fines can accrue. And then you have to pay the renewal fee.

For more information, go online and search for "P & C license" in your state and there will be plenty of state resources with all the requirements. However, you need to be clear about one thing.

Your license is your responsibility.

Sometimes there's an HR person or a claims licensing agent who will keep in contact with you and remind you about your license. That's great, but it's not required. You need to keep and do everything you need to do to maintain that license. Your license enables you to get a job in the field you've chosen, and that's a great thing.

The nice thing about becoming an adjuster and getting some experience is that you always have something to fall back on. I've worked as a writer and a playwright and worked on films and when I need to work as an adjuster, that's what I do. It's a good thing to keep in your pocket and it's not that expensive to maintain.

SUBROGATION, RESTITUTION, & TOTAL LOSS

In claims, I've referred to Collision and Comprehensive as "no fault" coverages. That's not exactly what is meant typically when one talks about true "no fault" systems, but in this case all I mean is that you can use them regardless of fault. But why? Why would you want to use Collision coverage, for example, if you weren't at fault?

Suppose you get struck by an at-fault driver and they have insurance, but their insurance is slow to take care of your vehicle. Maybe there is a problem confirming with their insured. Maybe they're just slow. Finally you get fed up and decide to turn to your insurance company. They will handle the loss, you pay your deductible, and then they will attempt to subrogate the other insurance.

Here's how it works: let's say the repairs to your vehicle are $2000 and your deductible is $500. You would pay the shop $500 and the insurance company would pay the rest, either direct to the shop or to you, or you and a lienholder. Maybe you get a rental car and the bill for that is $200. Your insurance company puts together a package and sends it, along with a demand letter, proof of payment, and estimates & photos, for the total amount:

$$\$1500 + \$500 \text{ (deductible)} + \$200 = \$2200.00$$

The process of requesting money paid out from the other insurance (sometimes called the adverse insurance) is **subrogation**. Insurance companies typically have whole departments dedicated to subrogation.

What about cases, however, like vandalism? If you recall, vandalism would be covered under the Comprehensive coverage. The only way you would really pursue the at-fault party is if they were arrested and prosecuted. What would happen is that the D.A.'s office will sent you a notice that the vandal is being prosecuted and asked to make restitution. At that point, you would send over the information they need to make the case – estimates and payment stubs, etc. Typically what happens is the perp agrees to pay $25 a month or whatever it is until they pay off the damage.

Most states require the insurance company to take care of the insured first – that is, the insured gets first money in subrogation or restitution cases. However, this varies depending on what state you happen to be working in. Generally, it's good business to do that anyway.

TOTAL LOSSES

These days, with modern cars being as expensive to repair as they are coupled with large crumple zones, total losses are quite coming. Normally, claims offices have people who handle all total losses, as they require some work. The most important thing to know is to be able to identify total losses from the beginning of a claim. That will help – there's no sense towing a vehicle to a body shop if it will never be repaired. Therefore the key is to get the vehicle moved to some sort of storage-free location as soon as possible.

Sometimes the vehicle will not be drivable but parked in front of someone's house. That is actually not so bad – you still want to get the vehicle moved ASAP, but at least there's no charges piling up.

If you suspect a vehicle is a total loss, if possible advise the insured to get all of their personal items out of the vehicle. Also mention to them it might not be a bad idea to start looking for a new vehicle now, and ask about any lienholder information or Gap Insurance. Gap insurance covers the difference between a total loss value and the amount owed on a loan.

Wait a minute – an insurance company won't pay off your loan?

It might. Or it might not. The thing about cars is, unless they were driven by Steve McQueen or Batman, they are a **depreciating asset**. That means **cars go down in value**, not up, except in rare cases. Sentimental value doesn't count. The fact that your grandmother bought you the 1987 Tercel means about as much as the love you had for your dead mangy mutt. Claims is not a sentimental business. The issue is how much would somebody pay for the item in question.

Whether a car is a total loss or not is generally not a negotiable issue. It's typically done via the numbers – once damage gets to a certain percentage of the value of the car, you're done. In some cases you could have a "constructive total" – a total which may not reach precisely the numbers, but when you add up the rental costs and probable supplements, it doesn't make sense to repair the car.

There are also other kinds of totals. A vehicle caught in a flood is an automatic total loss if the water gets up to touch the dash. Reason being, once water touches the computer, you will never be able to repair the car and guarantee that no problems will arise. In fact, often unscrupulous people will often take flood cars from one state and move them to another state, get them registered with a clean title, and then sell them to the public.

The values for a total loss are typically calculated through a third-party vendor. There are some common ones, like Mitchell or CCC. Some companies still use NADA books to get a value, but this is a very imprecise way to obtain a good number. The advantage of a third-party vendor is that they do a market survey beginning with the zip code of where the vehicle was purchased, meaning they get closer to the real value. They even, if available, provide dealer or private sale quotes where the person can replace their vehicle if they want to.

Insurance companies don't often use Kelly Blue Book however. Those values are designed for dealerships, which have overhead – employees, a showroom, etc. Those numbers will almost always be higher because of this, and so customers will want to use them.

As I mentioned before, cars depreciate. And not everybody is good at negotiating a deal. The fact is, most people have bad credit, don't do a lot of research when buying a car, and get talked into more vehicle than they can afford by car salesmen. (If you think I'm being harsh, I'm not. It's like Vegas. You think they built all those fancy hotels losing to customers? Or the lottery – if everybody broke even with lottery tickets, nobody would ever win any money. All sales systems – and you can think deeply about this if you want to – *require lots of losers to a relatively small ratio of winners.* In other words, if car salesmen couldn't get you into more car than you can afford, there wouldn't be any car salesmen.)

Point is, a lot of people are going to owe more money on their car loan than the actual cash value (sometimes abbreviated ACV) of their car. There is a term for this in the industry: "upside down." If you are **upside down** in your car, it means you don't have enough value to cover your loan.

What happens then?

Hopefully they have gap insurance. If not, you are going to end up paying some part of their loan, and their only option is typically going to be to roll that money into a new loan for a new vehicle. Which means they will be even further in the hole.

SALVAGE RETENTION

So whenever there is a total loss, and we are paying for it, the insurance company is, in essence, buying the car. We literally take possession, stick it in a storage lot, and change the title out to be in the insurance company's name. At that point, we sell it for scrap. The amount we get back is the salvage value, which means that the insurance company makes some small percentage of their payout back. Meanwhile the car gets bought by somebody, usually for parts. There are whole business streams of resellers, people who use the surviving parts of damaged automobiles, refurbish the parts, and then sell them at a discount.

It's like being an organ donor. Except for cars.

Anyway, sometimes people will want to retain their total loss. It's legal in most states, but there are a few exceptions.

If someone retains their total loss, they get paid the value of the car (ACV) **minus the salvage value,** and they get to keep it. Sometimes they have to retitle the vehicle (obtain a salvage title) but not always.

The important thing to remember is that most of the problems that come out total losses have to do with communication. Keep the insured informed. Be polite, but don't lie to the customer. Doing that will help you iron out most of the problems with any claim, including total losses.

FINAL THOUGHTS

What I've tried to do in this book is lay out some of the main things you need to know when starting out as an adjuster. I wanted to give some inkling of what the job is really like, to let you see if this is something you want to undertake. The job has been good to me and I very much enjoy training and talking about liability, value, and other similar topics related to the job. And I've never regretted getting into this area some twenty years ago.

Now, because I am not using a specific contract, of course there are certain little details that won't be known until you actually begin working for a company. However, this will give you a head start on any sort of orientation or training you'd get in a claims class. And you'll be able to use some of this hopefully as a reference when you're pondering one liability decision or another.

There's always little things that you'll need to learn, including a computer system and whatever the specific procedures are for handling claims for the company you happen to work for. But with this in hand, you will be a little better prepared to deal with concepts of insurance and working as a claims adjuster. Once you've done it for a while, you may find that it suits you.

I have put some links at the website for this book which may come in handy for adjusters, including links to TDI and police report overlays and such. You can access these at:

www.autoclaimstepbystep.wordpress.com

Thanks, and good luck.

APPENDIX

RECORDED STATEMENT OUTLINE

Whenever you're taking a recorded statement, you have to listening actively at all times. You're not going to necessarily know all the right questions to ask, because the person you are interviewing is going to give you information that you need to follow up on. What follows below is a basic template that should represent the minimum information required.

*Questions begin after you do your **standard introduction**.*

BASIC INFORMATION

Can you state your full name and spell your last name for me?
What is your address?
And your telephone number?
What is your driver's license number? Are there any restrictions on that license?
What is your telephone number? Any other numbers where we can contact you?
What is your date of birth?
And your social security number?

Thank you.

FACTS OF THE ACCIDENT

What was the date of the accident?
What was the weather like that day?
What time did it occur?
Where did this accident occur?
What road were you on?
How many lanes are on the road where you were traveling?
And what lane were you in?
What was your approximate speed?
What is the speed limit in that area?
Were there any traffic controls?
What direction were you facing?

What was the purpose of your trip?

What road was the other person on?

What lane were they in?

Were there any obstructions – did anything block your view?

Were there any injuries in the accident? (If yes, then obtain details of who was injured and how they were injured.)

Were there any child seats in the car?

Were there any witnesses to the accident?

Is there a police report?

Which police department responded?

What is the case number?

Was anyone cited that you know of (i.e., did anyone get a ticket?)

DAMAGES

What was the point of impact on your vehicle?

What was the point of impact on the other vehicle?

When did you first become aware of the other vehicle?

Were you or the other vehicle's driver able to take any evasive action?

Did your airbags deploy?

Did the other vehicle's airbags go off?

What were the positions of the vehicle after the

impact?
Were there any skid marks or debris left in the
road?
Was your vehicle drivable?
Was the other vehicle drivable?

THE NARRATIVE

Ask the interviewee to explain the accident you in
their own words
Ask follow up questions as necessary based on
what they tell you

AFTERMATH

Following the accident, did you speak with the
other driver(s)?
What was said?
Who do you think was at fault in the accident?
Why?

CLOSING

Thank you. Is there anything else you'd like to add
that I may have missed?
You did understand that this conversation was
being recorded, and I did have your permission to

do so?

All right, then at this point I am going to wrap this up. My name is ____, and it is approximately (TIME) on (DATE) and this will end the statement.

(Turn OFF recorder)

CLAIMS HANDLING GUIDELINES FOR TEXAS

Note: business days are normal working days (Monday through Friday without holidays) while calendar days are just that, calendar days. Also note that these are not all of the available claims handling guidelines; these are just the ones that will apply most often to entry-level claims.

Acknowledge all first-party claims within 15 business days

Begin investigation of first-party claims no later than the 15th day of receipt of notice of a claim

Request all necessary statements, forms, proofs of loss, etc., from first-party claimant no later than the 15th day of receipt of notice of a claim

Notify in writing the first-party claimant of acceptance or rejection of a claim, and if rejecting claim, provide an explanation no later than the 15th business day after all items required of the insured have been submitted (i.e., statements, forms, proofs of loss, etc.)

Requests for additional time to investigate the claim and determine if the insurance company will accept or reject the claim must be sent no later than the 15th business day after the date of receipt of all items required of the insured have been submitted

If additional time is requested, notify the first-party of the acceptance or rejection of a claim no later than the 45th day after the date of the initial notification

Pay first-party claim after notifying them the claim will be paid no later than the 5th business day after notice is made

Notify first-party insured in writing of initial offer to settle a third-party claim no later than the 10th day after the offer of settlement is made

Notify first-party insured in writing of settlement of a third-party claim no later than the 30th day after settlement is effected

STATUTES OF LIMITATION BY STATE

State	Property Damage	Bodily Injury
AL	6	2
AK	2	2
AZ	2	2
AR	3	3
CA	3	2
CO	2	3
CN	2	2
DE	2	2
DC	3	3
FL	4	4
GA	4	2
HI	2	2
ID	3	2
IL	5	2

State	Property Damage	Bodily Injury
IN	2	2
IO	5	2
KN	2	2
KY	3	1
LA	1	1
MN	6	2
MD	3	3
MA	3	3
MI	3	3
MN	6	2
MS	3	3
MO	5	5
MT	2	3
NC	3	3
ND	6	6
NE	4	4
NH	3	3
NJ	6	2
NM	4	3
NV	3	2
NY	3	3
OH	4	2
OK	2	2

State	Property Damage	Bodily Injury
OR	6	2
PA	2	2
RI	10	3
SC	3	3
SD	6	3
TN	3	1
TX	2	2
UT	3	4
VI	5	2
VT	3	3
WA	3	3
WI	6	3
WV	2	2
WY	4	4

ABOUT THE AUTHOR

Joseph E. Green has worked as a claims adjuster, supervisor, private investigator, and trainer since 1998. He lives with his wife, Dr. Faith Harper, and some very bad cats.